LONG MAY YOU RUN

A Baseball Saga

A Novel by Les Koenig

INTRODUCTION BY THE AUTHOR

In 1961, I was a 13-year-old boy living in Arverne, New York, a Queens suburb within a stone's throw to the beach. Baseball was in my blood, and even at that age, I wanted to coach younger kids. One day that Spring, I rode my bike twenty plus blocks to the A.C. Field, a massive open area with several backstops and infields where practices were taking place. I had been playing in the PAL for two years already, so I knew who ran the League - a man by the name of Mal Bodenlos. At that point, he didn't know me from a hole in the wall, but I already knew who he was - an animated man of Irish descent, his neck always red even though we were now months from summertime, reminiscent of 1950's-1960's Yankee infielder Gil MacDougald. Noticing his station wagon, I approached the area he was standing at. I'm not even sure I mentioned my name, but I told him I had a bunch of kids from Arverne that I'd liked to coach this year. Amazingly, he didn't hesitate for an instant and the next thing I knew, he handed me catcher's gear, two bats, some balls, and a batting helmet or two. All he asked for was my name and phone number. To this day, I don't know which astounded me more: That he so willingly agreed to let me manage a team, or how I got all that equipment home.

Thus began, as it has been said in that classic movie, "the beginning of a beautiful friendship". Once Mal knew your name, you felt as though you were in the innermost of circles. As my teenage years went by, I coached PAL baseball and basketball, and got to know Mal well. He was a postman by trade, and I would often walk with him on his route in Far Rockaway, where we would talk about many things. I would often help when he needed an umpire. Loved doing it, especially when that meant getting a lift in his car from one field to the other. Mal was the neighborhood celebrity, and here I was, by association, stepping out of his car and feeling much bigger than my then skinny frame. He was, underneath a rough exterior, a truly wonderful person, and he was a terrific listener. By my calculation, the PAL had at least 6 baseball divisions going on, with only three fields available to us: The main A.C. Field, an awfully maintained field (but we loved it anyway), the Far Rockaway High School field with the mound and base distances adjusted, and for the Senior League, the PAL used a Major League distance field in the Redfern Projects. In 1964, a gorgeous field was built near the Wavecrest area, originally named O'Donahue Field, which supplanted the old A.C. How

Mal kept track of everything, got all the many games in each day and how seamlessly it all appeared to run is to this day beyond me.

Words cannot adequately describe how unselfish he was, how he gave so much of his time to make sure we all were involved in sports. He was beloved by the entire community, and when I got a call in April of 1973 (I know the time frame because it was a few days after my daughter Traci was born) that he was being honored with a breakfast in Far Rock, without hesitation I accepted the invitation. They gave me the honor of asking me to speak, along with several others, including famed Far Rockaway High School Coach Jack Kerchman. Years later, after Mal had died, O'Donahue Field was renamed Mal Bodenlos Field, and nothing could have been more apropos. For, if ever anyone embodied the spirit and evocation of our youth, it was Mal. I would like to dedicate this book to him. Mal, long may your memory run.

FOREWORD

The scenes in my life go around in my head
All the pressure got to me, so my music was dead
It's a prelude to a story that took me years to write
The fire was already burning so why should I fight?

The bridge was wide open, the temptation was there
This night had the faith, so I went with a prayer
I'm searching for the captain to direct me right home
And disregarding the stranger that always kept me alone

I'm missing my younger days and know this song isn't over
There is something that I just need to say
Someday when I hang up my piano, I'll meet you on the field and together
we'll play

I find the will to go on, a little smile is all it takes
Come get your second wind and throw away your mistakes
If you only knew how hard it was to write this all down
I'm filled with deep inspiration to turn it around

In the coldness of each passing spring, it was just a matter of time
Somewhere in between the lines we knew it was never a crime
Serenaded the crowd who left with mementos and souvenirs
Through the turnstiles we danced and said goodbye to the passing years

I'm missing my younger days and know this song isn't over.
There is something that I just need to say
Someday when I hang up my piano, I'll meet you on the field and together
we'll play.

--WRITTEN BY DR. SCOTT KOENIG

Table of Contents

Chapter 1

Well, it doesn't get any bigger than this. Game 7 of Major League Baseball's World Series. The Detroit Tigers are nursing a 2-run lead in the top of the ninth over the NL Champion Atlanta Braves. There is no doubt who is being called on to close out the series, the Tigers' great reliever, Billy Jeffries. As Jeffries trots in from the bullpen, and his theme song ("In the Midnight Hour" by Wilson Pickett - an homage to his Dad's favorite song) pervades the ballpark, the crowd is on its collective feet. All narrow leads are tenuous, but this one is especially harrowing since it is as they say, "for all the marbles".

With the majority of the 52,416 fans capturing the moment on their cell phones, Jeffries completes his warmup throws. It has been another superb season for the veteran - now in his 15th and final year, and having already announced that he is retiring, he compiled 42 saves and an ERA of 1.98, plus making another All-Star team. The Tigers have relied on him in countless situations over the course of his career, but this is the chance to be champions. Jeffries has been at the top of his game throughout the postseason. Can he do it one more time?

Jeffries owns a blazing, live fastball, but his signature pitch is a devastating sinker which he throws at practically the same speed as his fastball. He normally has pinpoint control and if he gets ahead of a hitter, that sinker, tough on a batter to gauge, gives him a distinct advantage, especially when he would sometimes mix things up by just throwing the fastball. In other words, the hitter could not just look for the sinker and lay off it as it usually would cross the plate low and out of the strike zone. It could be the fastball coming, and the hitter must protect himself, especially with two strikes on him.

The moment might be too much for most pitchers, but Jeffries was primed for this chance to close it out. From Little League, throughout High School and College, and onto professional ball, it seemed the bigger the situation, the more he thrived. His ability to concentrate on the job at hand and not let the moment overtake him was among his many assets.

The first two batters went out rather easily, one on a tap back to the mound, the other striking out on one of those fierce sinkers. The crowd was in a frenzy - one more out, and the Tigers would have their first championship since 1984. But, as pitchers know, it is that final out that's the most difficult to get. Stepping up to the plate was the Braves' best hitter, Eduardo Lopez, the number 3 batter in the lineup, with clean up slugger Nick Shea on deck.

Lopez dug in. Jeffries took a deep breath and went to work. Carefully trying to move the ball in and out, the count went to 1 ball and 2 strikes. Jeffries noticed that Lopez was crowding the plate and wanted him not to be so comfortable, thus the idea was to waste a pitch by throwing it high and inside. He went into his windup and let it go, but the pitch sailed a little more inside than he wanted it to, and it nicked Lopez on the arm. Lopez trotted to first base, bringing Shea up as the potential tying run. As the home crowd groaned following the hit batsman, Jeffries turned his back towards home plate.

Curiously, his thoughts turned back to his youth, when a then reluctant version of himself hit a batter with a pitch in a championship game situation (a recurrence of a nightmare that had precluded him from pitching for several years in Little League), prompting a trip to the mound and a pep talk from his Little League coach, Lou Skinner. Mr. Skinner was able to calm Billy down, and get him to focus, striking out the league's most dangerous hitter for the title.

Now, he was able to drown out the crowd noise (albeit mostly cheering for him), and that memory from over 25 years ago was what he thought about as he smiled to himself and turned back towards the plate to get his catcher's sign. Paying scant attention to the runner Lopez (With a two run lead, his run meant nothing - only the batter mattered), Jeffries calmly worked the count in his favor, and on a 1-2 pitch, Shea whiffed at one of those great sinkers that dropped out of the strike zone, to end the hotly contested World Series, one that writers and players would call a Series for the ages.

In the jubilant locker room afterwards, lots of attention was being paid to Billy Jeffries, and deservedly so. If this was to indeed be his swan song, it was a glorious way to end it.

Repeatedly being asked what was on his mind as he was pitching in his final game, Billy, never one for self-promotion, simply said that he had a lot of people throughout his life who had prepared him for this moment. As he left to meet up with his family, Billy was a champion, and was able to leave the game he loved on top, both for himself and as a part of a championship team.

Chapter 2

Joey Harrison and Billy Jeffries were the best of boyhood friends. They played Little League Baseball and PAL Basketball together in LaRock, a section of Springtown, New York, vied against one another in seasons of Stratomatic Baseball, and shared many other interests. As teenagers, they could quote lines from Poltergeist, Back to The Future, Goonies, and Raiders of The Lost Ark. They developed a mutual love for not only Van Halen and Run DMC, but for Classic Rock music as well, no doubt chips off the old block (of their parents) - Beatles, Motown, Doors, Neil Young, Bob Dylan, Otis Redding, etc.

By the time they were entering Springtown High School, Billy and Joey had reputations and it was a foregone conclusion they would both make the Varsity Baseball team. That they each shined in their 3 seasons is an understatement. Billy, playing centerfield when he wasn't pitching, was the star of the team, and had his pick of colleges, all offering athletic scholarships. He chose the University of Miami because of his desire to play year-round, while wanting to stay on the East Coast. Joey also garnered several athletic scholarships, and chose UCLA, due to their storied history of excellent baseball programs and perennial trips to the NCAA tournament.

Whereas Billy enjoyed continued success (still playing both CF and Pitching) as a Miami Hurricane and was a first round draft pick of the Detroit Tigers, Joey was not as fortunate. Playing in an intramural basketball game at UCLA following a brilliant first season of baseball, he suffered an awful injury to his leg during a fall. He had the best medical assistance and enough time to rehab but was never the same player again. While he did finish out his collegiate career he never got even a whiff of an offer from the pros. Billy and Joey tried to stay in touch during those college years, but different time zones, distance, team travel, and schoolwork made it increasingly difficult, even before Joey's injury. When Billy heard about what had happened to Joey, he did speak to him, but the usually affable Joey seemed distant, and the conversations over time became less frequent, and at some point, there was no contact at all.

Billy played minor league ball for a few years, and the Tiger organization began grooming him as a pitcher, while still allowing him to play in the field.

The biggest decision was whether to make Billy exclusively an everyday player, or a pitcher, as he excelled at both. If both, would it be easier to slot him into a starting pitcher's role, so he would take the mound every fifth day, and play the field (or DH) on the other days? Or, were his skills better suited to being a closer, and if so, how would that jibe with him hitting, since a reliever never knew when he would be pitching?

For a historical comparison, the great Babe Ruth multi-tasked for 2 seasons as a member of the Boston Red Sox: 1918 (a 13-7 record, 20 starts on the mound, 2.22 ERA plus a 2-0 record in the World Series, while batting .300 in 95 games as an outfielder, 382 plate appearances, leading the league with 11 home runs {in the so-called dead ball era} and a .555 slugging percentage), and 1919 (a 9-5 record, 17 starts, 2.97 ERA, plus 130 games and 543 plate appearances as a hitter, .322 batting average, leading the league in 4 major categories - 29 home runs, 103 runs scored, 113 RBI's, .657 slugging percentage). Eventually, after his trade to the Yankees, it was decided that his skill set would be better served by making him an everyday player, and the rest of course is history.

Ultimately, although the choice was a difficult one to make, the Tigers felt that Billy would be most successful as a closer. In an era when even top starting pitchers seldom were going the distance, the role of a top notch closer, who projected to be consistently great over a span of seasons, was becoming more and more critical to a team's success. The big ballclub realized they would be sacrificing the opportunity of utilizing his bat on an everyday basis, but this decision was one that over time could not be questioned, as he became the premier closer in all of baseball.

Joey, on the other hand, went back to settle in his hometown of Springtown, NY, became a productive salesman and married his college sweetheart. Yet, he never was able to let go of how close he came to living his boyhood dream of playing in the Major Leagues. The struggles he continued to have in the aftermath of his unrealized potential while providing for his family (he was now a father of two) were about to be tested in a way he could have never imagined.

Chapter 3

On a mid-August night, the following year after Billy had retired, he heard his cell phone ringing. Recognizing the caller, he picked up.

"Hey, cousin," said Billy.

"How are you doing, Billy?" replied his cousin Ronald Carson. "I hope I didn't catch you at a bad time."

"Never a wrong time to hear from you, Ronald. How's the family?"

"We're all good, my man. Everybody OK at your end? How's retirement treating you?"

"Yeah, we're all fine. I do miss the competition, the camaraderie, but I don't miss the travel and being away from home for so many months."

"Well, you went out on your terms and got that elusive championship."

"Yep, that's true. What a spectacular victory parade in Detroit. I got to admit, with all those winter banquets, I put on a few pounds, but it was all great."

"Hey, Billy, do you think you'll make it home for Thanksgiving this year? Not only will your folks be thrilled, so will your sister-in-law and your favorite nephew."

"Count on it, Ronald. I've already spoken to Shandra as well as your favorite niece Jada and nephew Jamal, and they are excited. Of course, that would have to include a trip to Manhattan and some Joe's Pizza."

"Of course. Although you remember Vinnie, right? His Italian restaurant in Springtown has great pizza too."

"Wouldn't want to get Vinnie mad. Even after all these years, I always remember it's better to be on his side. Vinnie was really, underneath all that bravado, a great guy and a damn good catcher."

"Hey, there's another reason for my call. This one's tough. You may want to sit down."

"Ronald, it's not anything bad about my folks, is it? I spoke to them last week and they seemed fine."

"No, they are both doing great. OK, here goes. It's so hard for me to say this, so let me just say it quickly. Lou Skinner died."

"Mr. Skinner? Oh, my god, what happened? I mean, he had to be what, in his early 60's?"

"62 to be exact. Sudden heart attack. The town is in a state of shock. I can only imagine what his wife and family are going through. Anyway, the funeral is in two days. I just thought you needed to know."

"Needed to know? Of course. Email me the details. I'll grab a flight east tomorrow."

"That would be amazing, Billy. Let me know your flight and I'll pick you up. Assume you'll stay with your parents?"

"Yeah, guess so. Hey, Ronald, I just can't believe it. Lou Skinner - what a great guy. I'll see you tomorrow. Let me tell Shandra and I'll book a flight."

"OK, Billy, I'll email you right now."

"Thanks, Ronald. See you. Man - Lou Skinner."

As he hung up the phone, Billy's thoughts immediately went back to his childhood, and how Lou Skinner, his Little League coach, taught him so many valuable life lessons, shaping Billy into becoming the man he was today. Billy had resisted pitching in his youth, owing to an earlier time when a few years prior, he hit a few batters, and could not get past it. This was despite his team, the Mets, needing a pitcher that could handle pressure situations.

In the final championship game, Billy was left with no choice and volunteered to pitch. There was a trip to the mound by Lou Skinner at a pivotal point in that game which set Billy on a course that would not only be a life lesson, but a career path. Think of a teacher or any adult for that matter who influenced you in the formative years in a positive way, so much so that decades later, that person can bring a smile to your face. Well, Lou Skinner was a teacher - a teacher of how to play the game the right way, and a man who could inspire. No doubt I must be there to pay my respects in person, thought Billy. No doubt at all.

Chapter 4

Ronald put calls into some of his childhood teammates who no longer lived in Springtown. Al Gustafson was now an actor, living in Manhattan. Al was a heartthrob who never let his good looks get in the way of his competitiveness on the field. George Porter, now a college professor at Northwestern in Chicago, always seemed to be wise and mature beyond his years, and it was no shock that he followed a path of academia. Kenny "Ike" Eichorn, a salesman living in Pennsylvania, one of the heroes of their team. Each of them had only one thing in mind - when was the funeral, and what was the address? They would all be there.

Some of the old gang, like Ronald, stayed in Springtown: Joey Harrison, their popular shortstop who loved baseball. Vinnie Panzini their catcher, verbose and combative for sure but could back it up on the field. Paul Dodsworth, their "tenth man", who compiled all of the team stats, and was as much a part of the team as any of the players. Ronald got in touch with each of them as well just in case they hadn't heard about Lou Skinner; all of course said they would be there. Not the way he would have wanted a team reunion after all these years, thought Ronald, but it will be great to see everyone. He hoped those who are coming from out of town will at least stay overnight so we can all get together. Mr. Skinner would have liked that.

Chapter 5

On a gorgeous, sunlit August day, an overflow crowd filtered into the Springtown Memorial Chapel. Seated in the front row was the immediate family, all understandably grief stricken, accepting sincere condolences from many before the service began. There was Lou's wife Lisa, their children Peter and Amy, and Peter's kids Emma age 11 and Bobby age 8. Also, in attendance among the multitude were the one-time teammates under Lou's tutelage: Vinnie, Al, George, Ike, and Paul who sat near each other after having reunited outside the chapel. Joey arrived a little later and was several rows back. Billy did not want his celebrity status to overtake the proceedings, so he and his parents arrived late with Ronald and sat in the back.

Among those who spoke was Paul Dodsworth.

"I met Lou Skinner when I was 11 years old and to say he impacted me in a positive way is the understatement of the century. As much as I loved baseball, I was not 'player material' and so I just decided to become the team's number one fan, going to all the games so I could watch my friends play. Lou took notice of me and asked if I would like to become the team's bench coach and statistician, an opportunity that I jumped at. From that moment, my confidence and sense of productive achievement skyrocketed. To feel as though you truly belong especially at such an impressionable age meant everything to me. Sure, I would get teased from time to time, especially from Vinnie who is here today (leading to many at the gathering chuckling), but I knew in my heart that I was really a part of the team. Lou's teams did not always win, but they were always the most prepared and fundamentally sound. His philosophy was simple - stay even keeled, enjoy yourself, and be able to look in the mirror and know that you gave it your all. No matter what the score was or the team's place in the standings."

"As I got older and the days of Little League were behind us all, I stayed in touch with Lou. He coached for a few more years, then took over the reins of league commissioner from Jake Collins who retired to Florida. I would help with scheduling and other league matters, at least until I went away to college. Even being away, we spoke on the phone often. You can say I had long since become his biggest fan. When I came home for the summer, we would get together and talk about baseball and life, mostly in that order. After college, I stayed in Springtown and started coaching teams - younger ones first, starting out in tee ball. I'm not sure which I liked better - the coaching itself, or on days when our team wasn't playing, helping Lou put down the chalk lines and perhaps being a base umpire if needed. From an adult perspective, I witnessed firsthand how unselfish and giving Lou Skinner was. To be able to juggle his work schedule with running the League, and to never, ever complain that he had too much on his plate, well, he continued to be my inspiration. I suppose there are people in towns across the country, men and women who give up their time for positive yet unselfish reasons. Well, Lou Skinner was ours. I look at the multitude of people here today. Why, there is not among us a life he didn't touch, and for those who could not be here today, I know their sentiments are the same. The only thing he loved more than baseball was his beautiful family. He was taken from us way too soon, and in conclusion, I'd have to say that the imprint he has left on everyone he came in touch with is larger than life. People like Lou Skinner don't win Nobel Peace Prizes or get featured on 60 Minutes. But I would like to think that he was as deserving as anyone. Guess you can say he was, to quote one of my favorite movies: 'Almost Famous'. So long, Coach, and may you rest in peace."

After the service and the succeeding procession to the funeral, Billy came over to Joey. They hugged.

"Hey, Joey. Been a long time. Good to see you, even on such a sad day."

"Yeah, great to see you too Billy. I am so proud of what you accomplished. I tried to watch Tiger games whenever I could and of course the post season. You were tremendous."

"Thanks, buddy. I guess I owe a lot of it to Lou Skinner. I hope this won't upset you too much, but I often dreamed of us being in the majors together, maybe even on the same team. After high school and even while you were at UCLA, you were certainly on that sort of trajectory."

"Well, that's all in the past now, isn't it?" Joey said with unmistakable remorse.

Before either of them could say any more, the rest of the guys came over. In what seemed as though it were only yesterday, there was a lot of hugging to go around.

"Hey, Billy", said Al. "Can I get your autograph?"

Billy replied, grinning: "Sure, Al, but only if you give me yours. Just imagine, Gusto already in some major movies. How was it like working with Denzel?"

Laughing, Al replied. "Billy, I was only in two scenes in the movie, but I have to say, he was very nice to me. Seems like a straight up guy."

Vinnie spoke up. "Guys, I hate to interrupt this love fest but Dodsy and I were talking about how we should get together tonight for dinner. I happen to know a great Italian restaurant, wink-wink."

Dodsy added: "I'll text each of you out of town guys the address to Vinnie's place. Shall we make it 7 o'clock?"

They quickly agreed, and as they left the cemetery, they knew tonight would be special - lots of catching up to do, and much reminiscing. After they paid their final respects to Lisa Skinner and the rest of Lou's family and went to their respective cars, Billy couldn't help but think that, judging from Joey's body language, he may have hit a nerve. Getting into the SUV with his parents and Ronald and his family, he made a promise to himself not to bring it up to Joey tonight.

Billy called his wife Shandra when he got back to his parents' house, after the service.

"Hey, honey, I know it had to be a tough day, but it must have been great seeing the guys."

"Yeah, it was, and we're going to get together in a little while for dinner. Should be great reminiscing. Must tell you, though, despite the embrace, it was a tad awkward talking to Joey. I think I may have touched a raw nerve when I mentioned something."

"What was that?"

"I told him that my dream was for the both of us to be in the big leagues, and perhaps even play for the same franchise. I sensed his feeling of self-pity. I don't think it's jealousy, Joey is not that way. He even went out of his way to tell me he watched as many of my games over the years as he could. I suppose he feels unfulfilled. Anyway, I won't bring it up again."

"I get it, Billy. Let's hope the other guys don't steer too much of the conversation towards your career."

"If I have anything to do with it, I'll try to get them to focus on our Little League days, and maybe shift the convo to Al and his acting career. Plus, there will be some glass raising for Mr. Skinner. Anyway, got to run. Looks like Ronald is ready to leave. Tell the kids I love them and will talk to them tomorrow. Good night, babe. We're still on the same page with what we talked about earlier, right?"

"Absolutely. Have a great time tonight, Billy. Love you."

Chapter 6

Tucked away, considerably off the main thoroughfare in town, was the Italian restaurant known as Vincente's, owned by Vinnie. He never left Springtown, and had bought the place several years ago, when it was previously known as Gino's Pizzeria. He kept the original place intact and built a fine dining section with a great reputation. Vinnie was a hands-on owner, always with a handshake to greet his regular patrons. Although he was going to take the night off to be with his childhood friends, he made sure he had his A-team staff on hand for the evening. He worried a little about customers potentially hounding Billy for a photo op and/or autograph so he decided to close the fine dining area down and make it private dining for the gang.

As the guys came strolling in, they were quickly escorted to the rear. Vinnie made sure they knew that dinner was his treat but asked that they tip the staff generously. As though it had only been 25 minutes rather than over 25 years, the conversation was free flowing. They decided to get the food and drinks ordering out of the way, because otherwise, they would never get around to it.

George Porter started the conversation off. "I don't know about you guys, but I still think about our Mets team a lot, especially the year we won it all. I know that I'm supposed to focus on my students, but being in Chicago where the winters can be brutal, as soon as the weather gets nicer, I wish I was 12 years old again, and I daydream about being out there playing with you guys. I do believe that because the competition was so strong, especially among the better teams, what we had to overcome to win made it even more enjoyable and unforgettable. One more thing - For those of us who played high school ball, seeing Mr. Skinner there in the stands, cheering us on, well, I know it meant a lot to him to see his proteges there, and for sure it meant a lot to me."

Ike Eichorn chimed in. "I'm a salesman and being on the road in my car a lot, I listen to baseball games and sports talk radio. Sure, some of us had success on the diamond through high school, and of course it goes without saying how proud I am to tell people I was Billy's teammate, but it's true, Georgie.......er, can we still call you Georgie, or are we supposed to be more formal these days? (George gestured at that point, as if to say, no problem).

Yep, it's true, I think of our team all the time, and how lucky we were to have Mr. Skinner as our manager. What a great guy."

"I would like to propose a toast," Al Gustafson shouted. "To Lou Skinner. I know, Mr. Skinner, you would love to be here, seeing your students of the game again after all these years. You may physically not be here, but you'll always be in our hearts. You meant so much to us and we are all better for having known you."

A chorus of "Lou Skinner" was bellowed out by the contingent.

Paul Dodsworth was next. "Guys, with so many of you having to travel a long way to get here, it meant a lot, not only to me, but to Lisa and the rest of the Skinner family. I don't know too many people who could have made the kind of impact Lou did. As one who stayed in touch with him, I can vouch for the fact that he never changed. He treated the game with respect, and especially as commissioner took tremendous pride in overseeing and mentoring kids at their most impressionable age."

"So, what about you, Joey?" Said Al. "What have you been up to? I know that after high school, you went to UCLA and I did hear about your accident; bummer. How has life been treating you?"

Joey sighed, and to try and stay positive, had this to say: "Well, sure, I miss the game and of course those Little League experiences are great memories. I wound up moving back to Springtown, took over my dad's sales business, attempted to stay in shape by playing softball on Sundays, and have kids of my own now to live vicariously through on the ball field."

Vinnie, never one to stay silent for too long, spoke now. "Guys, do you remember how we beat those Pirates for the championship? I would say there are two things that I distinctly recall: Joey's unreal catch on that short fly ball, and Billy's relief job to close the season out, striking out the annoying Bruce Plank. While I know it didn't work out for you, Joey, as you would have wanted, think about it, guys, Billy's career really started then. I got to tell you, Billy, I play fantasy baseball every year, and in the beginning, it was an unspoken, unofficial rule that only I could draft you on my team, but as the years went by and you got better and better, it was tougher to get the others to agree. Anybody else play fantasy?"

Ronald added: "You think you had issues with that, Vinnie? Man, he's my cousin. Not only did I have to go through hell on my league's draft night, but the constant requests for his John Hancock were through the roof. Not that I'm complaining, though, especially last year when the Tigers won it all with Billy on the mound. Lots of pride involved."

"I think we all shared that pride, Ronald," said George.

Vinnie, as outspoken as he had been back in the day, said: "Hey, Joey, let's recreate the scene of your great catch. Dodsy, correct me if I'm wrong, but it's the final game of the best of three for the title. I believe it was in the fourth inning, we're already down by a run, and I think it was Jason Satriano who loops a ball into short left field, and he's running hard and is thinking double all the way, but Joey is running equally hard and at a 45 degree angle, his back to home plate, he gets to the ball, rolls over, and holds onto it. I don't know about you guys, but I felt we were going to win right after that."

"You have great recall, Vinnie," said Dodsy.

"Er, thanks, Vinnie," added Joey, "but we don't win it without Billy's relief job."

Billy, sensing that Joey would want to deflect attention away from him, tried to steer the conversation in a different direction. "You guys know what I loved the most about our championship - well, besides those beautiful trophies, that is. Those Pirates may have had the stronger team at least on paper, but Mr. Skinner really coached us on the fundamentals, and it was so cool to see all our hard work paying off. Dodsy, remember the famous play he taught us with runners on first and third?"

"What was that? I can't recall," uttered Gusto.

Dodsy explained to Al. "You should remember Al, because you were on the mound once when we successfully pulled it off. We called it "The Cutoff Play". In Little League, as you will recollect, the pitcher does not go to the stretch with runners on and by the same token, base runners cannot take a lead and move off the base they occupy until the ball passes home plate."

"45 feet from the mound to home plate and 60 feet from base to base, right Dodsy?" blurted out Vinnie.

"46 feet to home actually," corrected Dodsy. "So, there is usually not too much stealing, and runners generally advance only on passed balls or wild pitches, with one exception. If the team up at bat has runners at the corners, especially with less than two outs, they will send the runner from first because the other team would be afraid to make the throw all the way to second and have the runner on third run home to score. Well, Lou devised a play to countermand that. He would have Vinnie make a hard throw but not all the way to second. Instead, Vinnie would fire it over the pitcher's mound to Joey who had moved in from short, and Joey would be in a position to be able to fire it back to Vinnie to tag the runner from third who had instinctively thought Vinnie's throw was going all the way to second. It was such a cool play and Joey, correct me if I'm wrong, but we were 3 for 3 on the play that year."

"I guess you're right, Dodsy. We practiced it a lot. If nothing else, Mr. Skinner knew it kept all of us on our toes."

"Oh yeah, it's coming back to me now," said Al. "I mean, no teams ever did that in Little League. Just goes to show you how well he coached us. He really stressed defense, playing smart, and doing the little things that could make a difference in the outcome."

Ronald thought that the timing was right for some laughter. "Hey, Gusto, remember when you tripped over the first base bag while running to first in that final game?"

"Do I remember? I tell my peeps all the time that I'm the reason Billy became famous. If I didn't flip over the bag, hurt the leg, and had to be rushed to the hospital, Billy never would have relieved me. Everything happens for a reason, right?"

Maybe it was that last sentence, that things happen for a reason, but something made Joey feel regretful. He did appreciate Vinnie going out of his way to remind the fellas about the clutch catch, but it was unfortunately having a reverse effect on Joey, and he was the first to call it a night. "Guys, I've got to get up early for work tomorrow. Listen, Billy, Al, George, Ike: It was great seeing all of you. Let's try to stay in touch. Ronald, Dodsy, I'll see you around. Vinnie, great dinner and I'll see you too."

After Joey had left, George broke the silence. "What is wrong with Joey? Dodsy, is everything okay with him at home?"

"Guys, as you know, Joey and I were close when we were kids. Even in high school. But we went off to college, became adults, getting married and having kids, working at jobs, and we really don't hang out anymore. We call each other on our birthdays but that's about it. Wish I could be more insightful."

Billy added: "You know, I think it's a pretty known fact that Joey was my closest friend growing up. Baseball, basketball, Bobby Hull hockey, listening to music, playing Stratomatic, watching TV and going to the movies together - we did it all. We lost touch after his injury at UCLA, and it wasn't until today, after the funeral, when I came to the possible realization that his carrying the lost opportunity to take baseball to a pro level is what's eating at him. At least, that's the vibe I'm getting. I think we can all acknowledge his talent on the field and his love for the game. He ate, drank, and slept baseball from Little League through high school and I suspect that love never died. Anyway, that's my take on it."

The ex-teammates could do nothing other than nod their heads in unison. Wanting to maximize the remaining time to hear as much as they could about each other's lives, family and otherwise, they dropped the subject and stayed until about midnight when, as they proceeded to leave and made promises to stay in touch, Billy received a text message that would ultimately lead to a life change he could never have envisioned just a few days ago.

Chapter 7

The text Billy received was from Kimberly Harrison, Joey's wife. It read: "I know it's late, but please call me when you get this."

"Ronald, hang on a second. I just got a text from Kim Harrison to call her no matter what the hour."

"Hope it's nothing too serious. Sure, call her. I'll be outside, Billy."

Billy called Kim on her cell. Kim picked up immediately.

"Hi Billy. Thanks for calling. I got your number from your Dad."

"Sure, no problem, Kim. What's up?"

"Billy, Joey came home over an hour ago. I asked him about how the dinner went. He did everything he could to avoid me. He went up to the bedroom, came down a little while after that, and said he was going for a drive. He looked so distraught. I begged him to sit down and talk to me, but he stormed off. I have been texting him and calling him ever since; he is just not answering. Billy, I don't know where he is and frankly, for the past few days, he has shut me and the kids out. At first, I thought it was him being so saddened to have heard about Lou Skinner, but I just sense it is more than that. Billy, you were his best friend growing up. I was hoping that he would at least return your call. Can you give it a shot?"

"Of course, Kim. I'll let you know either way. Hey, Kim. Let me ask you this, and I don't mean to pry or overstep my boundaries, so stop me if I'm going into an area I shouldn't. Has Joey been happy? What I'm getting at is this; as a kid and all through high school, he was a levelheaded guy who kept things on an even keel. He was just so consistent in everything he did, especially on the ballfield. But there was also a certain bounce to his step, a lot of joy in his life. I have only seen him briefly today, but I get the sense that there is something nagging at him. I wonder if the leg injury in college and the end to what was perhaps a promising future for him has taken something out of him far more than he knows."

"Billy, you're very perceptive. We met in college, fell in love, and while the good times have greatly outweighed the bad, there will be moments when he will retreat to a dark place where he can be quite remote. I mean, he is a wonderful father and a loving husband. But sometimes I think he is just going through the motions at his job and, I hate to say this, at life in general. We don't really socialize with friends that much. I'm sure Paul told you that they barely speak anymore. We used to go on vacations as couples first, then as families when the kids came. I was hoping that the sight of all of you guys would snap him out of it but I'm guessing it had the reverse effect and it may be driving him further into some sort of abyss. Billy, please find him and see if you can talk to him. Please."

"Of course, I will, Kim. Keep your cell phone on. Look, Joey is too pragmatic to do anything drastic. I'll find him."

"Thanks Billy. Oh, by the way. Congratulations on the World Series. We watched every pitch."

"Thanks, Kim. I'll be in touch as soon as I know where he is."

Billy said a final goodnight to Vinnie, left the restaurant, and met Ronald in the street. He relayed to him the conversation he had had with Kim.

"Ronald, you drive us to your house and if you don't mind, I'll take the car and go hunting for Joey."

"Sure you don't want me to come, Billy?"

"Nah, it might be better one on one, assuming I find him."

"Where will you start looking?"

"I think I may know just the place."

"Well, text me when you find him. Hope he's OK."

"Will do. C'mon, let's get you home."

Chapter 8

Ronald drove home, as Billy put a call into Joey's cell but all he could do was leave a voice message. He texted him and that went unanswered as well. Billy plugged his phone into the car charger, sensing he might need it fully charged for what could be a long remainder of the evening. Except for visits on holidays and special birthdays, Billy had been gone from Springtown for well over a decade, but he still knew his way around.

After making sure that Joey had not hit any of the taverns that were open late (not there, thank goodness), his instincts led him to the sanctity of the Little League ballfield. As he pulled into the parking area, not surprisingly, he noticed a single car there. Must be Joey's, thought Billy, exhaling. Billy parked and walked over to the other car, to see if Joey was inside, perhaps sleeping. After seeing that the car had been vacated, he walked towards the field and as he approached, with a lamppost partially illuminating an otherwise dark ballfield, he saw the unmistakable silhouette of his childhood friend, a beer can in his hand, staring into space. Billy decided to call Kim right away to let her know he had found him. Joey didn't yet detect him, and so Billy decided to keep his voice to a whisper, resigned to the possibility that Joey might notice him and want to run off to continue to be alone.

"Kim, I found him. He's in the bleachers of the baseball field. I don't think he knows I'm here yet. I'll fill you in later; just wanted to let you know he appears fine. Do me a favor; text Ronald. I promised I'd let him know too. Do you have his cell number?"

"No, I don't. Please text it to me, Billy. Thank God you found him. Stay in touch."

"Will do, Kim."

As Billy approached the bleachers, Joey appeared almost disinterested as he shouted out: "Well, Mr. Sherlock Holmes, you found me. How'd you figure it out?"

"What do you think? You were drawn to your first love, the baseball field where you had the most fun. Going to the funeral conjured up those memories."

"Well, maybe my first love, but now I'm not so sure. Want a beer? I have an extra 4 or 6."

"Sure, I'll take one," replied Billy as he proceeded to sit next to Joey. "You know, Kim has been frantic in trying to reach you."

"I'm truly sorry about that, really I am. But I needed some alone time to try and sort things through and I was not in the mood for any lecturing."

"I called her as soon as I saw you here and told her you were okay. But, are you really okay?"

"Depends on your definition. Hey, Billy, I truly do not wish to lay anything heavy on you and then have you attempt to play amateur psychologist. After all, you are only here for a short time."

"You're not going to get off that easy, Joey. I've got all night and then some. Why don't you start from the beginning?"

Joey stared into Billy's eyes, and after a slight hesitation amid a feeling of awkwardness, began. "Okay, here goes. But do me a favor; let me get it all out, because it might be best for me to completely unburden myself with what I suppose has always been latent. No guilt here, mind you, but seeing all the guys and especially you triggered something in me."

"Got it Joey. I'll just listen."

"Funny, when we were kids, the deepest conversations we had were who or what was better - Brett or Schmidt, Bird or Magic, Back to The Future or Goonies, Springsteen or Billy Joel."

"Well, those were important to us then. Anyway, continue."

"Billy, I had a great childhood with many friends and loving parents. I received a good education at UCLA. I married a great girl. It was good spending time on the west coast just to see how the other half lives. I love Kim and my kids. I earn a decent living. So, guess you can say that I lucked out and am more fortunate than most people. But I don't think I've been the same person since the day I hurt my knee."

"Despite the good years in high school, and the scholarship, I knew my limitations. I was never the star prospect like I knew you would be. But I did want a chance. I loved the game so much, I was even willing to toil in the minor leagues, maybe get lucky and get a call up but if that didn't happen, I knew I would be okay with it, having given it my best shot. Maybe I'd get into coaching at the college level or maybe even higher up the ladder. I truly believe I would have been good with that. But, something in me died that day; I lost my desire. I even tried playing the next few seasons at UCLA, but the injury really took its toll. I was at a major baseball school and you can imagine the number of scouts at each game. I knew for the final two years; they were not seeing me at my best- I was a shell of what I once was. But seeing them chase down some of my teammates, well, it really stung."

"So, after graduation, we settled back here in Springtown. Kim has a good job teaching. My kids are healthy, thank god. The older one, Will, is 11 and plays Little League. He's pretty good, I must say. Plays shortstop and pitches, and yes, he's a much better pitcher than I was, though that's not saying much (Joey grins, Billy does too). My daughter Alexa is 5. She's a real daddy's girl - playing tee ball already. I play competitive modified fast pitch softball on Sundays, but like most things in my life, my heart just isn't in it. Believe me, I know, the odds of making it to the big leagues are slim and if you remember anything about me, you'll recall I preferred to deflect any accolades that were hurled my way. But, if I'm being totally honest, Billy, I played well enough in high school and at UCLA prior to the injury that I couldn't help but pinch myself and flirt with the idea that I actually had an opportunity at the game I love more than anything. I am far from a monster these days; I guess those thoughts are for the most part in the recesses of my mind. But, when I read about Mr. Skinner, then saw all the guys, especially you, I guess it brought everything to the forefront. I'm just not sure if I can make peace with myself and be happy. I don't want to drag Kim or my kids down with me; I just don't know what my purpose in life is. So, now that I have spilled my guts out.... I'm sure you regret coming to find me."

"Joey, I feel awful that we drifted apart when we went off to college. I wish I could have been there for you as a sounding board."

"Billy, you have no idea how many times I wanted to pick up the phone and call you. Part of it was my foolish pride coupled with the fact that you were not just a major leaguer, but a star. I don't mean that to sound jealous or envious, but I know what fame can do to someone. Even to someone like you."

"Joey, if you called, I would have been there in a heartbeat."

Joey, with tears streaming down his face, continued: "I have to admit, I do feel better getting it all out in the open. I miss our childhood and having you as my friend. It made me feel blessed; I haven't felt like that for a long time. I'm sorry - I hate unloading this on you, especially because it's been such a long time."

"No need to apologize, I'm glad we're talking now. Hey, do me a favor and call Kim right now. She's worried sick about you."

"Yeah, good idea. When do you go back to Michigan?"

"I want to talk to you about that, but first things first. Call your wife."

Joey took out his phone, saw the number of messages Kim had left, felt guilty about it, and dialed her back. Billy gave Joey some privacy by moving out of the bleachers to promenade around the perimeter. He looked out onto the field where it all started. With memories flooding back, he thought of the plan he was about to lay on Joey. It was either the best idea he'd ever had, or the worst - he could not be sure.

Joey hung up with Kim and moseyed over to where Billy was standing. "Hey, Joey, remember the way the semi-finals ended the year we won it?"

"Like it was yesterday," replied Joey. "The Reds were about to at least tie it up and probably win it. They had runners on second and third with one out in the last inning, the batter - I think it was Neil Golden, our high school teammate, smashed a drive into the right center field gap. The ball had game winning hit written all over it, but you came out of nowhere and made the catch. Ryan Billigan who was on second, breaks towards third at the crack of the bat, you fire it to me, I tag the base and the game is over. Seth Kammawitz had correctly tagged up and would have been the tying run, but the force out at second superseded that. Wait, why are you laughing so hard?"

"This is the first time I've seen you smile all day. Do you realize your recall of that play, some 25 or so years ago, is spot on? Admit it. You were never happier than when we were on the Lou Skinner Mets. That was the best time of your life. Look, I have an idea. I know the key to happiness isn't living in the past, but what if we could recreate it? Go back in time in some way?"

"What the heck are you talking about, Billy? Play an old timer's game?"

"Not exactly. Look, I had a talk with Dodsy yesterday. Did you know that Vinnie was managing the team this year, but got kicked out of the league for verbally abusing an umpire, and Dodsy, whose son David is on the team, took over? I mean, Ronald's son Lamar is also on the team, and he never even told me the story. Anyway, the second half of the season is about to start, and I took it upon myself to ask Dodsy if he wouldn't mind some help in coaching from the both of us."

"What do you mean, the both of us? You live in Michigan."

"Ann Arbor was great while I was playing for the Tigers. I could be home half of each season and catch my son's games. But, Shandra and I have been talking. Neither of us has family in Michigan. My parents are here in Springtown. Shandra's folks are a stone's throw away in New Jersey. I want to be closer to Ronald and his family. School doesn't start for another few weeks and Shandra has already spoken to someone at the Springtown Administration office. They've emailed the forms to her. What I'm saying is, Joey, we're moving back to Springtown. We'll stay with my folks until we find a place."

"Billy, this is crazy. Are you sure you aren't making a huge mistake coming back here? You're big time now. You're not doing this just for me, I hope."

"Not at all. I mean, coaching the team together would be the icing on the cake. I really want to rediscover my roots and raise my kids where I grew up. Plus, the pizza and Chinese food sucks in Ann Arbor."

"Yeah, I guess that's true," said Joey with a smile, so many thoughts racing through his head. "Well, I suppose that if you're turning your life upside down, it would be horrendous if I didn't go along with this. How's the team doing anyway?"

"From what Dodsy told me, they finished out of the top two spots during the first half of the season but were competitive. I think they were 5-5. But they are about to get some reinforcement."

"Um, I don't think they'll let us play, unless they have severely bent the age requirements."

"No, but Dodsy said they are short a player, and I can't wait to surprise the guys and introduce them to their newest teammate, one Jamal Jeffries."

"Ah, the prodigal son. Is he as good as his old man?"

"Well, for one thing, I made sure that at an early age, he would pitch. Couldn't watch him go through what I did back then. I got to admit, he's good."

"Okay, but can he also hit?"

"Like a young Hank Aaron, and he's fast - like his Uncle Ronald was."

"Too bad my son Will is a bit too young for this team. It would have been incredible to watch our boys play together. You know, I named him after you."

Billy was taken aback. "You did? Wow, what an honor. What made you decide to do that?"

"I wanted to give him the name of someone I always admired and respected. C'mon, let's go and get some sleep. I have to juggle some things around with work so my schedule can be cleared up for the team."

"I'll take this as a Yes, then."

"You, Dodsy, and me. Just like old times. The real Three Amigos."

The two friends hugged, got into their respective cars, and drove off, both their minds racing. Billy - about to be homeward bound and Joey, hoping to get a second chance.

Chapter 9

Joey walked into his house, his brain in overdrive despite the long day and late hour. Kim was in bed, but not asleep. Thank god it's still August and she doesn't have to go to work, thought Joey as he entered their bedroom. Anxiously awaiting what he had to say, Kim sat up, propped up by a few pillows, all ears. Starting out with a sincere apology to her, he related the events of the evening, in detail. Kim could not help but notice how enthusiastic Joey was; there was a buoyancy to him that she frankly had not seen in a long time.

When he was finished, all Kim could utter at first was "Wow". No need to harp on the fact that he had so much to be thankful for; she was intuitive enough to know that deep down he knew that, and a late night cliche-filled lecture was not the way to steer this discussion. Rather, she focused on the positive: "What an amazing person Billy is".......""That is so great, Joey - you, Billy, and Paul, just like old times".......""You'll make an amazing coach".......""Don't worry about Will's games on the days they conflict with the Mets' games; I'll be there for him."

Joey looked into Kim's beautiful hazel eyes, lovingly. He felt truly blessed.

"Thanks honey. I'll talk to Will in the morning; I should be able to make most of his games. I'll give Dodsy a call too. Got to get things in motion. I'm on such a high right now; I don't know if I'll get much sleep. Reminds me of my Little League days - that first practice in the Spring, the first game, playoff games: I hardly slept those nights and for sure, never needed my parents to wake me up."

"I'm so excited. I know I'm the love of your life, but I'm happy to share with your first love. Let's get to bed and tomorrow will be a new beginning for you."

"Thanks, Kim. Love you so much."

As Joey laid in bed that night, he pictured the final episode of his favorite TV show- Cheers. Norm Peterson reminds ex-jock Sam Malone about his one true love that he will always come back to. In Sam's case, the bar; for Joey, Little League. He finally closed his eyes, the reset button for him now pushed.

Chapter 10

The next day, at around noon, Billy gathered his family in the kitchen. His parents, Melvin and Claire were there, as well as Ronald and his family. He told them the big news - the Ann Arbor Jeffries' were relocating back to Springtown. It's a grandparent's dream to have family close in proximity to them and to watch their grandchildren grow up, and Claire could not hold back her tears of joy. Billy filled them in on his conversation with Joey, emphasizing that the move back was something he had been thinking about for a long time. Coaching with Joey would be the icing on the cake.

Melvin asked, "How does Shandra feel about this? Do the kids know yet?"

"Yes, Shandra is totally on the same page as me - her roots are on the East Coast too and she can't wait to get back. Don't get me wrong; she made a lot of friends in Ann Arbor, and is devastated to leave them, but with her personality, she'll find new ones here. Now, as far as the kids are concerned, I did have to do a lot more cajoling. Jamal was not happy at first and I was concerned. Now that I know there is an open roster spot on the team, and he can play alongside his cousin Lamar; he's all in. The fact that I'd be one of the coaches on the team is a bonus. As for Jada, I'm hoping that between soccer and tee ball, she'll meet some nice kids her age and let's not forget the fact that Joey's daughter Alexa is the same age as her."

Claire, always the overly cautious one, was about to blurt out that things are more expensive in New York vs. Michigan when she realized that money wouldn't be an issue for them. Billy had done well for himself and she was proud. These were not exactly the days Melvin used to tell her about, when pro-athletes needed off season jobs just to make ends meet. Major leaguers in the 21st century were now paid ridiculous sums of money. Filled with euphoria, she hugged her son.

"What's the timetable, Billy?"

"I'm flying back tomorrow morning, Dad. I need to take care of a few things, then the four of us will fly back here next week. Shandra has already taken care of registering the kids for school, and the house will immediately go on the market. If it's okay, we'll stay with you guys until we find a place. If we see something quick, we'll buy it; otherwise, we'll rent until we find what we want."

"You stay as long as you like; we have the room," beamed Claire.

"I may miss a practice or two; I think the second half of the season starts around September 10th. I'll have to check with Joey and Dodsy. Yes mom, before you ask - It's Paul or Mr. Dodsworth to the rest of the world, but always Dodsy to me."

Ronald chimed in: "This is blowing my mind. I must wrap my head around this. My cousin is back in Springtown!" Just then, Billy's cell phone rang.

"It's Shandra. Let me take this. Hey, honey. Yes, I just told my folks and Ronald the news. They are beyond excited."

"Billy, that's great. But listen, I was thinking. Really, there is no reason for you to fly back here only to turn around in a few days. I'll take care of everything. We can come back together to close on the house and see your friends to say goodbye, but please, stay put. I mean it; no worries."

"Are you sure? I can't fathom leaving you with all of that to do yourself; it's too much."

"100%. One of the nice perks of being married to Billy Jeffries is having the luxury of affording people to do some of this leg work. You just enjoy your family and I'll see you in about a week, OK? Love you."

"Love you too; talk to you tonight."

Billy gave the family the update. "Well, the only one who'll miss first practice will be Jamal. Guess I'll call Dodsy and see what's what. For tonight, I have a hankering for some New York Chinese food. Sound good?"

Laughter and high fives all around, as they watched Billy ascend the stairs up to his childhood bedroom, Melvin smiling to himself as he heard his son humming the opening bars of "Get Ready (cause here I come)", the old Temptations song.

Chapter 11

"Hey, Dodsy. How's it going?"

"Billy, great to hear from you. I just got off the phone with Joey. He sounds like a different person. We talked longer than we had for a long time. He was like the old Joey. He apologized for us not being closer these last several years, though I told him no apology was necessary. When you have a family and a job, it's hard to keep all the balls in the air. He didn't go into much detail about your conversation, but he asked if you guys could help me out with the team. I said to him, are you kidding? The two best ball players this town has seen. Billy, when you first mentioned it to me, I didn't think you were serious about it. You really are thinking about coming back to Springtown permanently?"

"More than thinking about it, Dodsy. We're officially putting the Ann Arbor place up for sale. I was originally flying home tomorrow to get everything set before coming back but Shandra insisted I stay right here, and that she would take care of it all and then fly here with the kids. The wheels are in motion! I do have one question, though- what do you think about Jamal? You said the team was short a player- is that still the case? I know the league can be pretty strict when it comes to roster size, and I would never ask you to drop anyone just for our sake."

"Well, as luck would have it, one of the kids on the team moved over the summer. There is a waiting list but since you are going to be an official member of the coaching staff, Jamal's name goes to the top of the list, so we're all set there. So, what can we expect from Jamal? Chip off the old block?"

"Plays third base and pitches, with a lot of hustle and heart. Hard to tell what's ahead for him but he's got the goods- at least for a 12-year-old."

"Great to hear. We can use all the ammunition we can get. Remember how good the Pirates were back in the day? Well, the players and coaches may have changed over the years but, wouldn't you know it, they are still the team to beat - they won the first half of the season."

"Ha, that's funny. Some things are constants in life. Do me a favor; email me the practice and game schedule, okay?"

"I'm one step ahead of you, Billy. Already in your In-Box."

"Hey, Dodsy. You still keep stats, like you used to?"

"Yeah, but no more calculating averages long division style and writing it out in pen. That's the beauty of the excel spreadsheet."

"I remember Vinnie always hounding you about his personal stats since we all knew you used lunch recess to update. What position does his son play?"

"Another like father, like son story. Vince Jr. is our catcher. Not as crazy and boisterous as his Dad, but a lot of fun to coach and watch play."

"With Vinnie kicked out of the league, do they let him attend games?"

"He can't sit in the bleachers and certainly not in our dugout, but you'll see him as his schedule permits planted behind the first base perimeter fence. He was kicked out of the last game of the first half, so this will not only be the start of the second half, but my first game as the official manager."

"Well, you know what they say? The best way to learn to swim is to get thrown into the deep end of the pool."

"Yeah, well let's hope I remember how to swim. Anyway, great talking to you, Billy and I'll see you at first practice. This is so exciting."

"For me too, Dodsy. Back to my roots, the way it should be. I'll see you soon."

After they hung up, Paul Dodsworth went down to his basement, opened a storage box covered in a layer of dust. He knew exactly what he was looking for. The scorebook he kept for Lou Skinner's Mets during their championship season and a special Billy Jeffries scrapbook where he kept baseball cards and articles of his friend throughout his career. These, along with the old trophy he was given as a "member" of the Mets, were his most prized possessions. He sat down and spent the next several hours poring over the books, smiling through tears of happiness as he leafed through the pages. Man, life has certainly taken a strange but awesome turn, he thought.

Chapter 12

The Mets division (12-13-years) was composed of the same six team names as when Billy and Joey last played - Pirates, Reds, Indians, Dodgers, Angels, and Mets. Springtown's Little League was rather unique. There were two halves to each season - Spring and Fall. The top 2 seeds in each half were considered playoff eligible. It was a rare event where the same teams finished first and second in both halves. It had only happened twice since the league went to a split season format in 1980. If the trend continued, the Pirates finishing first and the Dodgers finishing second in the Spring would mean other teams would be in the mix for the playoffs after completion of the Fall segment. There was a pecking order as to how the playoffs would work. The Pirates and Dodgers would be there, but the other four teams were working with a clean slate, all starting out 0-0. The Mets were 5-5 in the first half and had to at least get the second best record this half to contend. Based on experience, Dodsy figured they would need to go a minimum of 7-3. How were they going to make up at least 2 games this time? They would have to beat some very good teams along the way. Their 5-5 record left them tied for 3rd place in the Spring. Here were the first half won/loss records:

Pirates:	8-2
Dodgers:	7-3
Angels:	5-5
Mets:	5-5
Reds:	3-7
Indians:	2-8

Did this team have the necessary components to do that? Paul Dodsworth was deep in thought after returning his memorabilia into the storage chest. He hadn't seen Jamal Jeffries play, but if he was even remotely as good as Billy was, he would be a tremendous addition to the squad. Plus, according to Billy, his son could pitch, and pitching was the key to winning. Having Billy and Joey around to stress the fundamentals and impart their wisdom would be a big plus too. Paul could concentrate on things like putting together the batting order, subbing players in and out, emailing parents about any changes to practice days/times, and attending league meetings.

The first practice was only a few days away. If Jamal Jeffries was as good as advertised, he knew he would have to get some of his players on board by sacrificing some personal playing time for the good of the team. He knew how fragile egos could be, especially at their ages. Also, as low key as Billy seemed to be, he was still a real celebrity. They would no doubt be starstruck in the presence of one of MLB's biggest heroes. Paul chuckled, wondering if the boys would want actual instruction, or only autographs and photo ops? This might be a slippery slope - the last thing Paul (and Billy) needed was for this to go badly and for Joey to revert into his shell. It had apparently taken a lot for Billy to get through to Joey. This newfound joy could quickly take a turn and this time, there might not be a way to reverse it. He would have to hope for the best. With that, he went upstairs to talk to his son (and Met player) David. David would understand that they needed to focus, he was pretty sure of that. But how would the other kids react? He'd get a better sense after the team was assembled.

Chapter 13

Word traveled fast and within hours all the Met players knew what David Dodsworth knew: not only were there 2 new adult coaches to assist manager Paul Dodsworth, but one of them was the one and only Billy Jeffries. All of them were already keenly aware that Billy starred as a kid in Little League and High School in Springtown and retired as the best closer in Major League Baseball. Lamar Carson, being Billy's nephew, instinctively knew that his uncle would do everything to downplay his fame. But the others could not stop talking about it, whether to their families, guys on the other teams they'd run into, and amongst themselves. This was a big deal and the players had a lot of conflicting feelings. With Billy on site, this would be a chance to show off their skill and who wouldn't want to be praised by such a celebrity? On the other hand, Mets games would become a must-see for all walks of life in Springtown, from kids to adults. There would be added pressure. Regular season games are mostly attended only by the parents of the participants. Most keep one eye on the game but realistically, spend the time chatting about things having nothing to do with the actual game: forced socialization. Now, it would be different. They would be watching every move made by Billy Jeffries, and everyone would want face time with him. News reporters and photographers would suddenly appear, likely even out-of-town editions.

Billy was perceptive enough to realize the impact he was going to have and would do everything humanly possible to downplay his fame. It was a fine line to balance because the last thing he wanted was to appear cold and remote to anyone. He also had to contend with not wanting to steal any thunder from Dodsy as manager of the team. It had to be made clear to the players that Mr. Dodsworth was running this team, and that he and Joey were just there to help. On top of that, Billy had to safeguard against a possible downward spiral for Joey and whatever chasm he had fallen into. He needed Joey to remain positive, or his grandiose plan would have been for naught.

He decided to ask Joey and Dodsy to have a pre-practice breakfast on the premise of wanting to go over the roster and decide who among the three of them would be responsible for what. But most importantly, this get-together would be an attempt to test the waters on how his childhood friends were going to react to the potential circus atmosphere that was going to follow the team around for the entire Fall season. It was one thing, as Billy recalled, to stand in front of his locker day in and day out to field questions from reporters and other news media when he was a Tiger. As a Pro, there were other teammates to share the burden and they didn't care if Billy got the bulk of the attention. He put in calls to Joey and Dodsy. With first practice in two days at 10:00 AM, they would meet at the diner at 8:30 that morning.

Chapter 14

On a beautiful morning at the end of August, the three coaches arrived at the Springtown Diner around the same time. The diner was only about 10 minutes from the field, so working backwards, Paul figured they would leave around 9:40, get to the field, carry the equipment over from his car, and put out the bases. Not surprisingly, Paul already had a spreadsheet laid out on the table.

"I figured you'd like to see the first half stats. I also included the positions each played, highlighting in darker ink their primary positions. I'm old school, so I don't list WAR (Wins Above Replacement) or any of that other sabermetric stuff the pros use."

"Yeah, I never really understood what that meant anyway, even in the Big Leagues," added a chuckling Billy.

"Let's see the sheet, Dodsy," said Joey. As a kid, Joey loved pouring over the box scores from the previous pro games in the newspaper and was a keen student on the history of the game, which was rare to find among elite players like Joey was. Here were the salient stats of this edition of the Springtown Mets, for them to review:

NAME	POS	ABs	RUNs	HITS	2B	3B	HR	RBI	BB	AVERAGE
Vince Panzini	C, P	30	8	11	6	0	2	10	4	.367
Francisco Martinez	SS	31	10	11	6	1	1	8	4	.355
Elliot Markow	1B, P	29	7	10	5	0	2	10	3	.345
Ron Dent	CF	30	7	10	5	0	2	10	3	.333
Ryan Bernstein	P, RF	28	5	9	2	0	0	6	3	.321
Jacob White	LF, 3B	27	5	8	2	0	0	6	2	.296
Ben Calloway	2B, SS	27	5	8	1	1	0	6	4	.296
Lamar Carson	RF, 1B	22	5	6	1	0	0	3	9	.273

Hank Nielson	3B, C	30	4	7	1	0	0	2	2	.233
Warren Cameron	RF, CF	20	4	4	1	0	0	2	1	.200
Dennis O'Brien	2B, SS	20	4	4	0	0	0	2	2	.200
Robert LaChance	3B, LF	19	1	3	0	0	0	0	3	.158
David Dodsworth	RF, LF	14	2	2	0	0	0	0	3	.143
TOTALS		327	67	93	29	3	6	65	43	.284

"So, it looks like we have some pretty good hitters, though no one who really dominates. We of course want to form our own opinions, but anything or anyone that stands out to you, Dodsy?" asked Joey.

"Well, you're right about what the stats reveal. I would say that as a team, we need the most help in a few key areas: better defense, more timely hitting, and just a better general awareness of situational baseball. You guys will be tremendously helpful there."

"How's the pitching? I am guessing Ryan Bernstein is our number one starter, and I see you also show Vince Panzini and Elliot Markow as pitchers," Billy asked.

"Ryan is actually pretty good. What I like about him is his control. He doesn't have blazing speed but has a knack of getting ahead of the hitters. Elliot throws hard but frankly can be wild at times. Vince is more of an emergency late innings guy, when the others have reached their maximum allowed innings, or if we are involved in a blowout game either way. You remember the innings restrictions, guys, right?"

"If I remember correctly," said Joey, "it's six innings max a week and if you pitch more than three innings in a game, you cannot pitch for another 72 hours. Have I got that right?"

"You have a good memory, buddy. That's how it works, at least for the regular season. They tweak it for the playoffs, but we'll worry about that if the time comes."

"Well, I do believe we'll be able to make use of Jamal on the mound. His biggest problem is that he can lose focus, often in the early innings. It's something that he has to work through."

"That's great, Billy and I know you also said he plays third base," added Paul.

Joey spoke next. "There are three of us. So, we don't step on each other's toes, and we get the most out of the practices - how should we divide up the assignments?"

Billy wanted to approach this gingerly. "Of course, we can always change on the fly, but maybe we should start with Joey running fielding practice. I can throw batting practice, at least for now until we are comfortable with our own pitchers throwing BP. Joey, as practices continue, perhaps you work with the hitters on bunting and base running in general. Dodsy, of course, you will oversee the lineup and the in-game changes. I'm assuming everybody plays, like in the old days?"

"Correct on the playing rules. Everyone on your team must play a minimum of two innings and must bat at least once a game. Starters can go back in after those minimums have been met. I would normally look to sub in a bench player in around the third or fourth inning, allowing me the latitude to bring back the starters for the last inning or two. I'll let you make your own judgments, but Vince and Frankie normally play the entire game no matter what. Joey, I think you're going to love Frankie Martinez, since he plays shortstop. Great kid and a good all-around player. Anything else to discuss before we head out for practice?"

Billy was dreading this moment, but knew he needed to get it out of the way, lest there be the proverbial elephant in the room for the season. "Joey, remember when you and I went to baseball camp when we were 10 years old, and they brought in Willie Randolph as a guest speaker and to watch us play? I recall it like it was yesterday. It was unbelievable. Getting his autograph was the most exciting thing that had ever happened to me, and having his eyes on me and my teammates, giving us pointers, was a seminal moment. I noticed he stayed in the background because he didn't want to make us nervous. After a while, I forgot he was even there. Anyway, I bring this up because I am not naive to realize that my status, if you want to call it that, may potentially create a distraction. I will do everything possible to be low key and make it known that Mr. Dodsworth here is running the team; Joey and I are just going to help. As a new but old neighbor, I will have to walk a tightrope of not seeming cold and remote, yet not wanting to create a circus atmosphere. After all, I am not just visiting; I plan to live here for a long, long time." Laughing to himself, he added: "I think the kids will be pretty cool about it; it's the adults that I'll have to contend with. I've had experience with this in Ann Arbor; I'm telling you, after a while it will die down and I'll just be another member of Springtown. I can't stop whoever wants to make me any sort of distraction; I can only promise both of you that I won't be fueling the fire. I really just want to help and be a part of this team." Billy was mostly concerned about Joey's reaction, and sitting next to him in the booth, he tried to pick up on his energy.

"I think I speak for Dodsy when I say that we should be prepared for all of that, and we realize the burden will be mainly on you. There is a lot of maneuvering and posturing you'll have to do. You're right about one thing for sure - it'll be the parents, especially the fathers, who will be more pains in the neck, wanting that selfie with you, so they can frame it and hang it on their wall. Billy, from the moment you and I had our talk that night, whatever excess baggage I had been carrying around lifted away from me. I am as happy today as I was when we played together on the Mets. For the three of us, our key focus should be doing justice to the legacy of Mr. Skinner. Now, let's see if we can make this team a playoff contender."

Paul insisted on paying the bill, and after the three friends left the diner, there was a real buzz among the patrons. There were many who recognized Billy, but he didn't seem to notice.

As Paul got to his car and turned on the ignition, he wondered what kind of manager/coaches they would be. Over the years he witnessed many coaches striking fear in the players, barking out orders in an effort, he supposed, to exert their authority rather than keeping the team focused. It was clearly an ego thing for them. However, he had a front row seat to observe how Lou Skinner handled this responsibility. Lou was so beloved that his players would run through brick walls for him, and he never had to raise his voice. He got his message across with an even-tempered approach and a positive mindset. No matter how big the stakes, no matter how tense the game got, Lou never wavered in his demeanor. Paul likened him, from what he had read and what his dad told him, to Gil Hodges. Hodges in 1968 took a team that was the laughingstock of Major League Baseball since their inception, and turned them into pennant contenders and, shockingly, the Mets were the World Series champs in 1969. He too led by example, not by fear. It appears fate had bestowed the same team name to Lou's team, and now mine, thought Paul. He also felt certain that his style, as well as Billy's and Joey's, would emulate Lou's. "Bank on it" was Paul's last thought as he pulled up to the field.

Chapter 15

The three men, each in their own cars, pulled into the field parking lot at 9:50 sharp. Most of the players were already there. A few rushed over to Paul's car to help with the equipment, but each one's peripheral vision was directed towards the other two cars. Sensing their excitement, Paul motioned to the kids to drop the equipment right where they were, and waved Billy and Joey over.

"Boys, I'd like you to meet the two men who are going to be helping out with the team for the remainder of the season. This is Mr. Harrison and Mr. Jeffries."

"Hey guys. I'm Billy Jeffries" (as if they didn't know that) "and this is Joey Harrison. As Mr. Dodsworth mentioned, we'll be here to assist him. You may not know this, but Mr. Harrison and I wore the same uniform as you when we were your age. One year, we finished third, but the next year we won the Championship. We may not have had the most talent- that will forever be up for debate. But, our manager, Lou Skinner, stressed the fundamentals constantly. Mr. Skinner also preached teamwork and playing smart. That's what the three of us will be stressing in practices and games. We have no preconceived notions about any of you - everyone has a clean slate. We are also not going to fill your heads with too much; nothing drastic for now like changing batting stances or throwing motion. We'll have plenty of time to see you in action and help by tweaking things if need be. Joey, I'll turn it over to you."

"Thanks Billy. Guys, I'm sure you all know that Mr. Jeffries had a fantastic big-league career. But, let's try to remember that his greatness all the way from Little League and the other stops along his way to stardom was of his own doing. He will not be able to bat, field, or pitch for you. It will be each of you who will need to own your game and play up to your highest potential. As he mentioned and as you'll also hear from Mr. Dodsworth, we will be intensely focusing on the fundamentals. We will drill it into you, so you'll know how to respond in all sorts of in-game situations. You have our word that you can come to any of us at any given moment to discuss anything pertaining to the game. We want a team that is competitive, but always enjoying themselves. Paul, what do you want to add?"

"Guys, I realize that things have changed since the first half ended. You now have me for your manager, and two of the greatest ever to play in Springtown at your disposal. My greatest thrill as a kid was watching the two of them play. You'll find them totally approachable, and you are going to learn a lot. Now, if some of you can help carry the equipment over to the dugout, and put out the bases and pitching rubber, we can get rolling. We'll start off at these positions: Vince at Catcher, Elliot and Warren @ 1B, Ben & Dennis @ 2B, Frankie @ Short, Hank @ 3B, Jacob & David in Left, Ron and Robert in Center, Lamar & Ryan in Right."

Vince Panzini had something to say. "Hey, Mr. Dodsworth, with Bayer having moved away, have we filled his roster space yet?"

"As a matter of fact, we did, Vince. Mr. Jeffries' son Jamal is joining the team in a few days. He and the rest of the family are in the process of moving here from Michigan."

"What position does he play? Is he any good?" chimed in Hank Neilson.

Billy smiled, and replied: "Well, we'll let you see for yourself." Billy, not wanting to ruffle any feathers or show any favoritism added: "As for where he'll play, let's just say he can play all over, wherever he may be needed. He is excited to join this team, that I can tell you."

"Okay, Mets, let's take the field," shouted Paul. The kids each had a nice bounce to their step.

Joey, as they had agreed upon, handled the fielding practice, and he put the players through a brisk workout, starting off slowly, then gradually upping the tempo. He was pleased by what he saw- most of them had a lot of potential. He felt it was better to instruct as he went along. If an infielder was not in position to properly line up or receive a relay throw from the outfield, or if the right fielder did not back up first base on throws from any of the infielders or the catcher, it was quickly pointed out. Billy and Dodsy were each making mental notes of what they saw, so they along with Joey could converse later.

Towards the winding down of fielding practice, Billy called out to Ryan, Elliot, Vince, and Hank to come to the sidelines. Adjustments were made to the remaining fielders so all positions would be manned. Billy wanted to let the current members of the pitching staff throw; he had Ryan throwing to

Vince, and Elliot to Hank, and then Vince to Ryan. He instructed them to soft toss at first, then amp it up with velocity, encouraging them not to overthrow. He shared that he was more concerned with motion and control; the real heat, he told them, could come later. He witnessed what he anticipated after having heard Dodsy's "scouting report". Ryan had a nice easy motion, kept it simple, and was always near the strike zone. Billy could live with that- he probably won't strike many out, but he'll keep the fielders on their toes. As for Elliot, as advertised, he threw hard, but was often out of the strike zone. Maybe we could work on his mechanics, thought Billy, and if he took some miles off his fastball, maybe he'd be over the plate more. Billy had to chuckle to himself as he watched Vince. Just like his dad Vinnie all those years ago, he was not going to be more than a stop gap option. All, he felt, would be rectified when Jamal showed up. For now, he kept that under his hat.

Remembering that Lou Skinner loved throwing BP, keeping things moving along, Billy announced to the squad that he would be their "Iron Mike". He threw nice and easy. Dodsy thought to himself: Let them go home and tell their parents they batted against Billy Jeffries today, they would get a real thrill hearing about it. This setup also allowed Joey to watch the hitters from behind the back stop, while making mental notes.

From the first batter, Hank, and to those succeeding him, Joey told each player to lay a bunt down on the last swing and run it out. This kept the infielders awake and allowed Joey to see who could bunt and who couldn't. From what he saw, Joey realized this was an area they needed to focus on, knowing how valuable a well-placed bunt was at the right time in Little League games.

As practice was ending, parents who normally waited in their cars were predictably and anxiously trying to get near Billy. Billy did a lot of hand shaking and was glad to see the parents engaging Joey and Dodsy too so the three men could share the spotlight. A few parents did whip out their cell phones, and Billy accommodated each of them.

Dodsy reminded them of the next practice time. The first game was in less than two weeks. "Good workout today, boys. Let's build on it next time, okay?"

Paul, Joey, and Billy each felt great about their first practice, and promised to speak the next day about their early observations.

Chapter 16

Later that afternoon, Ryan Bernstein called Elliot Markow. They could not get over the fact that a real Major League star like Billy was going to be coaching them. Not only that, but he seemed like such a down to earth, relatable guy. They felt like any feedback from Billy, even in the form of criticism, would be welcome.

"I mean, this is not just a random adult telling us what to do; this is not even just any pro. This is Billy freaking Jeffries we're talking about. We have a coach who in a few years could be headed to Cooperstown."

"Yeah Ryan. Let's not forget that the other guy, Joey Harrison, was apparently a heck of a player in Little League and Mr. Dodsworth seems cool too. David told me his dad loves pouring over stats; he's like a real baseball geek, but in a good way."

Ben Caloway and Jacob White lived next door to each other. While playing Madden NFL at Jacob's house with Warren Cameron and Robert LaChance the four could not contain themselves. They couldn't wait to get their picture taken with Billy, and frame it. Kids that age don't normally plan out their future, but they had to be thinking about being able to tell anyone for the rest of their lives who their coach once was.

Similar conversations were taking place in all households of the Met players - calling and texting one another, or other friends and relatives. This was a big deal for all of them. Even the parents couldn't help themselves and were talking about it non-stop.

Chapter 17

While waiting for the call from Dodsy and Joey, Billy continued to worry about being too much of a distraction. As much as he would try to be a regular guy, he was not naive to believe everyone would treat him that way. However, any diversion would not be intentional, on his part.

Dodsy initiated the conference call with Joey and Billy. "So, how do you guys think it went?" he asked. Billy was glad that Joey spoke first.

"Well, we have to factor in that this was their first formal practice since the first half ended in June, so they were bound to be rusty. To me, they pretty much are what their record says they are, meaning I saw an equal number of pluses and minuses. On arm strength, the center fielder Ron looks good, and he can cover ground, so I'm confident he'll be able to get gap shots. Lamar in right has his dad's speed which will account for a lot, but he doesn't have a strong arm. Ryan looks comfortable out there which will be a plus for when he doesn't pitch. I thought Jacob in left had a good glove; we need to work with him on his throws as they are a little too arch-y."

"Vince has a live arm behind the plate, which will help on bunt attempts; with not much stealing at this level, I'm more concerned with his ability to frame pitches and minimize the number of passed balls. While he's no Pudge Rodriguez back there, he seems pretty good, and being his dad's backup catcher myself once, I can work with him. You were right, Dodsy, Frankie can really pick it and he has a gun for an arm. Elliot at first is agile enough, has good instincts as to when to move off the bag, and does what he can to get down and block low throws. As we know, it's a big foul territory, and throws past first can lead to an extra base, even two if there is a fast runner."

"I was frankly not that impressed with our third baseman, Hank. That is a demanding position; he's okay, but he seems a bit tentative. Billy, I'm hoping your son Jamal can be an upgrade there."

"The second baseman, his name is Ben, right? He'll be fine. I'll work with him on his lateral movements."

"As for hitting, I did see some good things. Vince can be a big-time slugger for us, Frankie has a quick bat, Elliot hits the ball hard, and Lamar will beat out his share of grounders. Ron, Ryan, and Jacob look to have some pop, Ben was hitting several nice line drives. I noticed Warren had a lazy bat but has some power potential. The others will need work, so we'll have to see how the next few practices and even the first game or two go. Billy, what do you think?"

"Guys, we know that pitching is the name of the game. Going back to our playing days here, we had two great starters in Georgie and Al. We could always count on a well-pitched game when either of those two were on the hill. Yeah, we could have used that third good arm for spot starting and for late inning work, but we all know the story there, ha. It's only the first practice and I warned the pitchers about overthrowing, so I could gauge only so much. Ryan has a nice easy motion, and you're so right, Dodsy, he will always be around the plate. Elliot, I can tell, will throw hard, but his mechanics are such that he will be difficult to count on in a big spot. I'll work with him, for sure, but I just don't know. Vince we can pretty much forget about; let's let him remain at the other end of the battery. So, that leaves us with Jamal. He's the new kid on the block and the coach's son so I want him to earn everything he has coming to him without any resentment. I can tell he will slot in nicely into the rotation and if he pitches to his capabilities as he did in Ann Arbor earlier this year, well, I have to say he could be a difference maker."

Dodsy loved what he was hearing. "Guys, this is better than I could have even dreamed. I distinctly remember like it was yesterday, listening to the way you guys dissected our games. You were both like Lou's mouth pieces. And, I can't forget about how you would break down what we were watching on TV, or the times our folks would take us to the Bronx to watch the Yanks or to Flushing for Mets games. You guys were beyond your years then, and the way you are analyzing things now, after just one practice, tells me that whether the team struggles or not, it won't be because of a lack of awareness. Hey, one last thing, on a personal note. I know David is not much of a ballplayer, although he sure is better than I was, not that it's saying much. Give me your honest assessment. Joey, believe me, I can take it."

Joey as a teammate back in the day, and now as a coach, always tried to find the positive in a fellow team member, and this time was no different. "Dodsy, I couldn't help but notice that his name was at the very bottom of the stat sheet. But I must tell you, he swung the bat with good authority, and I liked his stance. As for fielding, I know we already have a few second basemen, but he may be more suited to that position than the outfield. With the requirement to get every kid some playing time, we'll have to see how it all pans out."

"I'm going to tell him you thought he had a live bat, Joey. Coming from you, that will mean a lot."

"Dodsy," added Billy. "Don't forget. I was the one pitching to him and I agree with Joey. He does have a nice bat and good plate awareness. He'll be fine."

"Hey, thanks guys. Do you want to meet at the diner again before the next practice?"

They both agreed and ended the call. There was still much to do to get the team ready, but it was great to get the first one out of the way and to hear each other's feedback.

Chapter 18

Baseball practice, like all team sports, can get monotonous after a while. The more perceptive coaches will try to make them as fun and interesting as possible, while making sure the players work on fundamentals, stay sharp, and try to improve upon their deficiencies. They will often sprinkle in foot races or even choose-up games, with the coaches manning some of the positions to field all positions. Right before the first game, they may even schedule a scrimmage game against an opponent.

For the Mets, any practice doldrums were offset by the arrival of Jamal Jeffries. Here is where being the son of a famous ball player worked in everyone's favor. The kids went out of their way to welcome Jamal, even Hank who it seemed was destined to have his playing time at third reduced when Jamal wasn't pitching. It was not long before Jamal felt comfortable around everyone, not just his cousin Lamar.

Jamal, to put it mildly, proceeded to wow everyone, including Joey and Paul, with his glovework at third, his quick bat at the plate, and his obvious live arm on the mound. The Met kids knew they had added an important piece to their puzzle and could not wait until the second season started.

Paul had not changed much from when he would keep score of Lou Skinner's teams. He loved to pour over statistics. He knew what strategic advice to impart to an always receptive Lou, such as how to position the fielders based on who was up and/or who was pitching for the Mets, which of the opposition were more likely to lay down a bunt, stuff like that. It was not much different now, except that he was (pinching himself) going to be the final word, after running everything by Billy and Joey. He had a few ideas that he needed to throw out, so he suggested they meet for lunch the day before the games were to start.

"Guys, I think I'm pretty set on the lineup for the first game. I'm going to pitch Ryan and start Jamal at third, and the plan would be to pitch Jamal in game 2 the next day. My thought process is to let Jamal settle into the new surroundings, new league, etc. I'm thinking Vince behind the plate, Elliot, Ben, Frankie, Jamal across the infield, Jacob, Ron, Lamar across the outfield. Billy, I have two questions about Jamal: Did he have his heart set on pitching the first game, and, as the season progresses, has he had any outfield experience? I'm just worried about getting Hank enough playing time; he has a tendency to get down on himself and now that he will be relegated to a sub's role for at least half of the games, I wonder about his psyche."

"Dodsy, let me answer your second question first. When Jamal was 5 or 6 years old, I would tell him to trot out to the outfield and I'd hit fungoes to him. He could even at that age get to every ball and catch it, and he had an accurate arm. He wound up at third base early on in his Little League; I guess his coach felt that was where he was most needed. Safe to say, wherever you put Jamal on the diamond, he'll do the job. As for when he pitches, you'll have no trouble from him, I can assure you. In fact, he spoke to me after the last practice, not wanting to ruffle any feathers."

Joey added: "I can talk to Hank. I do sense that even though he is not shy about opening his mouth, he has a sensitive side to him. I'll explain that it's a reasonably long season, and that if he applies himself, he will see a significant amount of playing time. I'll also work hard with him on his fielding. All that being said, at any given time, we will have five kids on the bench and I'd hate for it to come off as though I'm taking Hank under my wing at the expense of others."

"Thanks, guys. I'll work on the batting order tonight and contemplate the subbing patterns as well. Joey, do you remember how we would spend the night before a game?"

"You mean, Stratomatic baseball? I used to love it. Billy, do you remember? I had that ritual with Dodsy during the season, whereas you and I played it in the winter months."

"Like it was yesterday, Joey. You know, I heard they have the game online now. Know anything about that, Dodsy?"

"Duh, I play it with David all the time. Nothing much has changed versus when we were kids, except I made sure to get the Detroit Tiger team so I could bring you in to close out my games."

"How did I do?," laughed Billy.

LONG MAY YOU RUN

"Like money in the bank. You would put the batters to sleep, like the classic song they always played in Comerica Park announcing your entry into the game - In the Midnight Hour."

"Yeah, my Dad's favorite song of all time. When I was young, if I had trouble sleeping at night, he would come into my bedroom and would make sure to set that song up for me to play on my Sony Walkman. Not your usual lullaby and it drove my mom crazy, but the lyrics fit, right? Toss-up between which version I'd have the Tigers play - the Wilson Pickett original, or the Rascals cover version. Love both versions, as does my Dad."

Dodsy added: "My dad told me that after Yankee games starting in the 1980's, they would play the Sinatra version of "New York, New York" after wins and the Liza Minelli version after losses, but eventually just did Sinatra's all of the time. I like the way you had them change it up, Billy."

"Maybe we can get a Strato league going if not now, after the season," said Joey. "I mean, what else do we have to do that's more important? Job, raising a family, chores, social calendar?"

"Sounds good to me," replied Paul. Our game is the second one tomorrow, which starts at noon. No opening day parade like in the Spring, so I just told the boys to be at the field by 11:30. Guess that's it; have a good rest of the day and see you there tomorrow."

Joey had a feeling that, when he got to the field ultra-early to watch the first game, he would see Dodsy there too, although maybe not Billy because of the latter's notoriety. Turns out, he was half right.

Chapter 19

"Didn't expect to see you here this early, Billy," remarked Joey as he made his way up the bleachers to where he and Paul were already sitting at just before 10AM.

"I just figured, the sooner I try to show I'm just another parent/coach, the sooner I'm hoping I can just blend in. I did want to get a look at the Pirates, since they play in the first game, plus their opponent is the Angels who we play tomorrow, so I'm just doing some advanced scouting."

Paul added: "That's my thinking as well, especially concerning the Angels. I did have a front row seat during the Spring season, but now I have to view things from a different perspective, and love having the extra four eyes here with me."

The Met hierarchy was treated to a good game. Making a lot of notes, mostly mental, they witnessed a high scoring contest, with the Pirates prevailing 10-7. Paul was able to remember that one of the 4 Angel pitchers used today, albeit for only one inning, was their #2 Starter in the Spring season, Fred Peters. Pointing him out to Billy and Joey, he mentioned that likely, it would be Peters who they would be facing tomorrow, as he was eligible to pitch up to 5 innings.

As it approached 11:30, they left the bleachers to head to the practice field to meet the team. The Mets were the home team, so they would begin the game on the field. Gathering them around, Paul read the starting lineup aloud:

Ben Caloway 2B
Jamal Jeffries 3B
Francisco Martinez SS
Vince Panzini C
Elliot Markow 1B
Ron Dent CF
Ryan Bernstein P
Jacob White LF
Lamar Carson RF

After a quick pregame workout, Paul decided to let Joey speak to the team, to get them pumped up. No matter if you are playing or coaching, there is nothing like the anticipation of the first game, and for Joey, it was no different than when he was a Little Leaguer himself. He kept his pep talk short and sweet.

"Guys, remember what we've practiced in the field, you always need to know the game situation and say to yourself, what will I do when the ball is hit to me? Be alert out there, and back each other up. When we are up, relax at the plate, and if you are on base, always know how many outs there are. Billy, anything to add?"

"I think you covered it. I'll just remind you to line up throws from the outfield like we worked on, whether it's Elliot or anyone else at first. Ryan, back up third or home on hits to the outfield, depending on where the runners are. No matter what the score, play hard and always have fun. Don't let a bad At Bat deter you from giving it your all in the field. There are many ways you can help the ballclub. Paul?"

"Nothing else to add. Mr. Harrison will coach third, Mr. Jeffries will coach first. Look to either one for the bunt sign or the take sign; however, if you want to bunt on your own for a base hit rather than as a sacrifice, that's fine, but please do not attempt a bunt with two strikes, since a foul ball will result in a strikeout. Let's have a good game." Huddled up, they all yelled out a resounding "Let's Go Mets", and the starters hit the field.

Ryan Bernstein was on his game from the get-go. Three up and three down in the top of the first, all on ground balls, one each to Ben, Frankie, and Jamal. In the home half of the first, Ben faked a few bunts off Reds pitcher Don Gellman, and was able to work out a walk. That brought up Jamal, with a buzz in the crowd for the son of Billy Jeffries. Jamal did justify the murmur, lashing a 1-0 pitch to deep left, but it was corralled by the left fielder who had been correctly positioned to play deep. Frankie was next and on a 2-1 count, he lined a base hit to center, Ben stopping at second. That brought up cleanup batter Vince Panzini. Working the count in his favor, Vince sent a 3-1 pitch over the center fielder's head. Both runners initially had to wait to see if the ball would be caught, but with Joey screaming for them to go, Ben was able to score easily, Frankie to third, with Vince pulling in at second with an RBI double. Consecutive singles by Elliot, Ron, and Ryan followed, and before the inning was over, the Mets had staked Ryan to a 4-0 lead.

Ryan was not striking out many, but he was getting the Reds to ground out or pop up and was ahead in the count with most batters. With a safe lead of 8-1 going into the last inning, and even getting some nice contributions from the bench, Paul decided to relieve Ryan with Elliot, to get the latter some work in a non-pressure appearance. Elliot did not have a good start, walking the first batter. But, when the smoke cleared, he had done okay, allowing 2 runs, and getting the last two outs via his flame throwing fastball.

Final score Mets 8, Reds 3

"Great game, guys," said Paul in the dugout. I liked the hustle and game smarts. We looked crisp out there. We have the early game tomorrow, so let's get here by 9:30."

Joey and Billy knew not to make sweeping generalizations after just one game, especially with what would likely be one of the weaker opponents, but it sure felt good to get that first win. Billy's thoughts quickly turned to tomorrow's contest against the Angels, with Jamal taking the ball.

Chapter 20

Paul knew the Angels would be one of the teams the Mets would have to beat out to qualify for the playoffs. They were a scrappy, yet inconsistent bunch, much like the Mets were. The tall, lanky southpaw Fred Peters was eligible to pitch up to five innings today. Peters' height and arm length worked to his advantage, as the ball seemed to get to home plate quickly, a young version perhaps of Randy Johnson. Paul did not want to overload his team by giving them too much to think about, but he did impart to his would-be bunters like Ben and Lamar that Peters' throwing motion would have him end up angling towards the third base side, and if they could push their bunts towards first, they would have a good chance of beating it out for a hit. Billy and Joey had only witnessed the one Angels game yesterday, but Joey felt strongly that their hitters 1 through 5 in the lineup were aggressive and would swing early in the count. He cautioned the fielders to get ready for some quick action. Jamal meanwhile was on the first base side, warming up with Vince. Vince had gotten the opportunity to catch him in practice, so he had some frame of reference for how he threw, but he knew that facing live competition was an entirely different matter.

The Mets were the visiting team today. Paul had to juggle the lineup a bit because Jamal was on the mound. Wanting to keep Ryan's bat in the lineup for what figured to be a low scoring affair, he decided to gamble and start him at third, over Hank. Paul told Hank he would get sufficient playing time there as well today. Being the first game of the day, many of the noontime players were spectators, wanting to get a look at Jamal on the hill. As the game unfolded, Peters proved to be a force to be reckoned with. He fanned Ben, got Jamal on a hard comebacker, and induced Frankie to pop up. In the bottom half of the first, Jamal was also hitting his stride. Throwing considerably hard, the Angels were not getting around him, and they went down in order too, strikeout, shallow fly ball to Ron, grounder to Elliot.

From there, the innings breezed by. Who would break the ice first? It was the Angels. In the bottom of the fourth in a scoreless duel, the number two batter Al Pierson grounded a seeing eye single up the middle. Jamal had been around the plate all day, but he uncorked a wild pitch to the next batter Jimmy Sadowski, sending Pierson to second and into scoring position. A 3-2 pitch to Sadowski was a tad outside, granting him a base on balls. Two on, nobody out. That brought up the cleanup batter, Sammy Bilkins. It also brought Billy to the mound to talk to Jamal as well as his infielders, Lamar, Dennis, Frankie, and Hank. Dismissing the unlikeliness of a sacrifice bunt (something a cleanup batter would rarely do), Billy told his guys (most of them substitutes) to play back and at least make sure of one out. As for Jamal, he stressed the importance of forgetting about the runners and to concentrate on the batter. They all nodded, Billy trotting back. Billy barely got back to the dugout when Bilkins, first ball swinging, placed one between short and third. Hank made a great play to get to and spear the ball on one hop, and had time to go to second for a force but was slightly off balance from having lunged for the ball, and saw his throw sail over Dennis' head into right field. Pierson scored standing up, and Sadowski attempted to do the same, but a great throw by Ryan, now in right, nailed him, Vince applying the tag. Bilkins did take second on the throw, but he stayed put, as Jamal recovered nicely to strike out the next two batters.

Hank came off the field, head down. Joey took him aside and told him he should be proud of himself, that not many players could have even gotten to that ball, and an off-balance throw was to be expected in that spot. He added that he much preferred an error of commission rather than an error of omission. "Your head was in the right place, Hank. The play is to get the force at second rather than try to settle for the sure out at first. You made a fine play on a tough ball. You don't get to that ball, it's at least bases loaded and no outs, and possibly the lead runner scores as our outfielders were positioned deep against that guy." Hank gave Joey a long look, seeming to take his coach's explanation to heart, and felt better.

David Dodsworth was the leadoff batter in the top of the fifth, and he went down quietly on a soft grounder to second. That brought up Hank, and wanting to atone for his error, tried pushing a bunt between the mound and first base. But he didn't place it far enough, and catcher Sadowski pounced on it. Hank had good speed though and Sadowski's hurried throw was in the dirt; Hank, hearing Billy yell to dig hard, was safe at first. That brought up another speedster, Lamar Carson. Peters, knowing this was his last inning on the mound, put something extra on his deliveries, and Lamar became a strikeout victim. Dennis was next, but he tapped back to the box for the third out.

The Angels could mount nothing further against Jamal in their half of the fifth, so the Mets came up for their last licks, needing a run to tie, and with the meat of their order coming up. They would be facing Angels' ace Juan

Navarro, yesterday's starter. Navarro had not fared well against the Pirates and was looking for redemption today. Jamal waited to see a strike and on a 2-1 pitch, laced a sharp single to left. Joey motioned Frankie over to his coaching box for a word. "Frankie, I doubt if they think we'll be asking you to bunt, but I just wanted to perhaps plant that seed. I want you swinging away. Be aggressive, be smart up there."

With Jamal primed to advance, Frankie dug in, and with the count 1-1, he sent a screaming line drive to center field. But, on a fine play by Pierson, the ball was caught. Jamal was running hard on contact, and it was all he could do just to get back to first safely. Tough break, as at worst, the Mets would have had runners on second and third. Vince was next, but on a 2-2 count, he foul tipped it into Sadowski's glove for out number 2. When Elliot followed with an easy fly ball to left, the game was suddenly over. A heart-breaking 1-0 loss, but a loss just the same.

In the dugout, the two coaches applauded the effort of the team, and made sure to mention that sometimes, when the opposing pitchers throw a gem, you just tip your hat. Reminding them that practice would be Tuesday, with games on Thursday and Sunday next week, Paul chimed in with some positive slants on the effort.

Paul said goodbye to Billy and Joey, and as he and David got into their car, he had a few thoughts: Jamal pitched great and with him, Ryan, and Elliot, we could be in real good shape, pitching wise. A 1-1 start was not that bad, but if they were to wind up 7-3 or better, they could ill afford another tough loss like this, especially when, based on the Spring season, the Pirates and the Dodgers were even stronger.

Chapter 21

With the formidable Pirates and the Dodgers both on their schedule this week, the coaches put the Met team through a vigorous workout session at Tuesday's practice. They broke off into two groups. Joey took charge of the infielders, working on situational plays while giving each infielder plenty of grounders and popups. Billy worked with the outfielders on positioning and throwing. Billy threw BP, with harder tosses this time. Before practice was over, under the careful watch of all three coaches, Ryan, Jamal, and Elliot threw on the sidelines, to keep them fresh. It was a good workout; they had the boys primed to square off against the two elite teams.

Thursday at 6pm rolled around, and the game against the Pirates was about to begin. Billy and Joey wondered if their old nemesis from their playing days, Bruce Plank, would make an appearance. Paul, cracking up, let them know Plank had moved away after finishing college. Based on Paul's scouting report, it was decided that with the Pirates being the more aggressive, stronger hitting team, harder throwing Jamal would start tonight, with Ryan going against the Dodgers on Sunday. Although the aura surrounding Billy Jeffries was beginning to die down a little as the folks in the town were becoming accustomed to his presence, there was still an unusually big crowd on hand, giving the contest a playoff-like atmosphere. They were treated to a dramatic game.

The Mets were the home team and although Jamal was giving it everything he had from the start, the Pirates' hard-hitting reputation came to fruition and they struck early. With one out, Bobby Baylor and Steven Lynch stroked back to back singles, and cleanup batter Rich Ortega drove them both home with a one hopper to the fence in left center. Ron's throw to Frankie who in turn fired home to Vince was just a tad late as Lynch slid safely across the plate.

Jamal appeared to be shaken by this sudden outburst of hitting. Whether in Ann Arbor or here, he was not accustomed to such a barrage. Billy decided to let him work out of it on his own and did not leave the dugout. Jamal did indeed get out of the jam, inducing the next batter Alvin Bean to pop up to second, and then fanning Gerald Linton to end the top of the inning.

Frank Carruthers was the Pirate pitcher and Paul had seen enough of him to know that he seemed to get the job done every time he took the mound. But the Mets were ready for him this evening. Ben beat out a slow roller to third for a hit, Jamal singled between short and third, and after a passed ball advanced both runners, Frankie, going the other way, singled to right. With no outs, Ben easily scored, and Joey held Jamal at third, but with the throw from the outfield going all the way to home, Frankie alertly scampered to second. Pirate manager Dan Murchinson made a quick trip to the mound.

It was early in the game, so Murchinson decided to have Carruthers pitch to Vince even though first base was open. He told him to pitch carefully and try to get him to chase a ball out of the strike zone. Vince was a bit overanxious, and swung at what should have been a ball, but got enough of it to send a fly ball to center. Jamal tagged up and scored as the throw went to third, keeping Frankie at second. However, he didn't stay there long as Elliot lined a shot just fair over third for a double and Frankie scored easily to put the Mets in front. Ron drew a base on balls, and when Ryan also walked, it brought up Jacob White to the plate with the bases loaded. On a 1-1 pitch, Jacob caught everyone including Joey off guard by laying down a beauty of a bunt down third. The Pirates could only hope that it rolled foul, but it stayed on the infield grass for a hit, Elliot scoring the fourth run of the inning. Carruthers came back to strike out Lamar and induce Ben to ground out to end a wild first inning with the Mets up 4-2.

Baseball can be a funny game sometimes. Just when you would have thought this would be a high scoring contest after the first inning blitz, both Jamal and Carruthers settled into a groove and after four innings, each team traded just one additional run. As the game moved into the fifth, the score was 5-3 Mets. Jamal was really bringing it, and after he caught the first two Pirates looking at called strike threes, Bobby Baylor tapped one back to the box for out number three.

In the Mets dugout, as they prepared to bat in the bottom of the fifth, there were a few decisions to make. Assuming the Mets didn't bust open the game now, should they keep Jamal on the mound, or move him to third where he was defensively superior to Hank? If they made that move, did they trust Elliot in a big spot? It was decided they would stay with Jamal.

The Mets threatened but did not score, and Jamal took the mound, facing Pirate batters 3-4-5. Steve Lynch made a bid for an extra base hit, but his drive to right center was hauled in by the speedy Lamar, with dad Ronald in the stands whooping it up. But Jamal was not as fortunate with slugger Rich Ortega who smashed a base hit just out of Frankie's reach. With the Pirate bench alive, Jamal prepared to face Alvin Bean. Bean hit a hard grounder to third, where Hank corralled it, steadied himself as he had been working on with Joey, and made a strong, accurate throw to Ben for the force at second. Two out now, and Joey could not suppress a smile in the dugout. When Gerald Linton struck out on a perfectly placed pitch by Jamal, the Mets were victorious.

In any season, some wins, even if they don't count for more than one, can feel like it, and this was one of those. When things settled down in the dugout, Billy, right out of Lou Skinner's playbook, reminded them to stay levelheaded, with another tough game up next against the Dodgers. As the kids left, even Billy knew this one was extra special.

Chapter 22

Sunday's game would be a family affair for Billy. He drove Jamal, Shandra, Jada, and Shandra's parents, who had come up from New Jersey for the game. Billy's parents would meet them at the field.

Joey also had a full car with Kim and the kids in tow. Fortunately for Joey, Will's game on the adjacent field was scheduled for 2 PM, following the Mets contest. Will was having a fine start to his season, and his team was also 2-1. Poised to become a Met next year, he was anxious to watch the older kids play. On the drive over, Kim said she wanted to invite Billy, Shandra, and the kids over for dinner that night. Between school, homework, and Little League, she wanted Will and Jamal to get to know each other off the field. The soccer season had not started, and Alexa had only been briefly introduced to Jada. Kim said she would check with Shandra, since she knew her parents were here for the day and could be staying for dinner, so there might have to be a plan B for a get-together.

The Mets were the visitors today, with Ryan on the mound, and Elliot poised to relieve him if necessary. The Dodgers, like the Mets were 2-1; since they finished 2nd in the first half, they were assured a postseason berth, but had their sights set on either winning the 2nd half, or at least keeping another team out of a playoff slot. They had 3 good pitchers, Ron Walston, son of the team manager Al, Bill Jones, and Ken Whelan. All threw hard and had good control of the strike zone. They were a well-coached team, relying more on pitching, hence their usual low scoring games. Jones was set to take the mound today, with Walston available for up to 4 innings and Whelan up to 2.

With the score tied at one in the top of the 4th, Jones uncharacteristically walked David Dodsworth, and hit Robert LaChance on the arm, putting two baserunners on and no outs. Dennis O'Brien followed with a nicely placed sacrifice bunt, putting runners at 2nd and 3rd with one out. No chance of intentionally walking Jamal Jeffries, with Frankie Martinez and Vince Panzini to follow, felt manager Al Walston, but he did pay a trip to the mound to let Jones know to pitch him carefully. On a 1-1 pitch, Jones placed the ball down low in the zone, but Jamal excited his family as well as his teammates by lining the ball into right center. As he slid into second safely, two runs scored, and the Mets were up 3-1. Frankie then lofted one deep to center, Jamal tagging up and going to third after Dave Willis' catch. However, the hopes for the Mets adding another run died with Vince grounding out to short.

Ryan kept the Dodgers at bay for the next two innings, although he was constantly working his way in and out of trouble. When he trotted out to the mound for the final inning to protect the two-run lead, Paul had Elliot, who had been removed earlier from the lineup, warm up on the sidelines in case Ryan faltered.

Leadoff man Ted Kalinsky grounded sharply to Frankie, who threw him out by two steps for the first out. But Gil Felson followed with a line shot over 3rd for a double. Dave Willis was next, and he stroked a ground ball single up the middle. Ron alertly allowed Felson to score and threw to second to keep the tying run Willis at first. Paul conferred with Billy who was warming Elliot up. They decided to bring in a fresh Elliot to relieve and face the Dodgers' cleanup hitter Torrey Jefferson. Jefferson was the Dodgers' one real slugging threat, and it was felt he would have a lesser chance with the hard throwing Elliot versus a tiring Ryan. Elliot had been working with Billy on his delivery; Billy wanted him to sacrifice a few miles off the fast ball in a tradeoff for strikes. But, sometimes, in the heat of a game and with a dangerous hitter up at a key moment, a youngster can get amped up and go away from that game plan, which is what happened on the first 2 pitches, both way off the plate. It was all Vince could do to extend and get his mitt on both pitches, to keep Willis at first. With Billy shouting at Elliot to ease up a bit as they had worked on, Elliot nodded and concentrated on his next delivery. This pitch was a good one, but so was the swing Jefferson put on it, a screaming liner to left that Jacob could just turn and face, as it went well over the fence for a game winning two run homer.

Jefferson crossed the plate and was mobbed by his teammates. The Mets walked off the field in utter shock. The first one to console a dejected Elliot was a gracious Ryan Bernstein, who blamed himself for having given up the hits and not leaving Elliot any wiggle room. The three Lou Skinner disciples, who had their share of excruciating back breaking losses even on route to a championship, knew they had to set the right tone, immediately.

As a player, Joey was the most even keeled, and he knew just what to say. "Guys, it was a tough loss today, but look at the big picture. We had a great win over the Pirates the other day, so, to use a tennis term, we held serve with the top two teams this week. Let's focus on the positive. With 6 games to go, we are right in the thick of things. We have shown we can go toe to toe with anyone. I also like the way our bench is performing. David and Robert, you gave us important at bats today, and Dennis, that was some bunt. Hey, you nearly beat it out. If we just keep practicing on the fundamentals, we'll be fine. We want to win every game of course, but speaking for Mr. Dodsworth and Mr. Jeffries, we are happy with the effort, and that is what counts the most."

Billy stepped in. "I echo all of that. Elliot, as a reliever myself, I always preferred to begin an inning rather than coming in from the bullpen during it. We put you in a very difficult position today and if we were going to lose the game on a home run, there's no shame in giving it up to the other team's slugger. So, lay the blame on us. In the future, we'll try to minimize your pitching appearances after the start of the inning. Dodsy?"

"Guys, I have seen real contenders wearing Met uniforms this week. Keep up the good work. Next practice is Thursday, since both our games are that weekend."

Joey left the field and walked over to watch Will's game, as Billy and Jamal headed over to the bleachers to gather their family, Billy shaking some hands along the way. Paul left with his wife Rebecca and David. His thoughts harkened back to when Lou would give a speech after a tough loss. Paul would look at the reaction of the players and he knew that Lou had said just the right things and set the correct tone. He sensed that the kids today mostly bought into everything Joey and Billy were saying. The way Billy deflected the loss away from Elliot was a master stroke. Joey, going out of his way to point out the positives he saw, especially signaling out the bench players was just brilliant. How they'd fare in the next 6 games would of course depend on performance, but Paul knew one thing - they would have the requisite confidence and preparedness, in droves, thanks to his all-star coaches.

Chapter 23

The Mets won their next 2 games against the Indians and the Reds. With 4 games to go in the regular season, they found themselves in a 3-way tie for first, with the Pirates and Dodgers. The Mets would have to overtake at least one of them to make the postseason. Current standings were as follows:

Mets: 4-2
Pirates: 4-2
Dodgers: 4-2
Angels: 3-3
Indians: 2-4
Reds: 1-5

Since the Pirates and Dodgers were still on the Mets' schedule, along with the Angels and Indians, they could not afford to lose both games against the top two. Even splitting games against them might not be enough. Plus, they could not take the Angels for granted, who beat them the first time and were a tough matchup.

The team assembled for a Friday practice the day before the Angels game, and the coaches decided to have some fun. Taking a page out of Lou Skinner's playbook, they went through a drill where the team lined up to the rear of home plate, in front of the backstop. One by one, a player would have his glove on and position himself right in the middle. Joey would be facing him, ball in hand, and would throw grounders to either side of the player. The player would have to field the ball, throw it back to Joey as quickly as he could, and then hustle back to the middle. After a few easy rollers tossed by Joey, alternating which side he threw the ball, he would then elevate into deceptive mode, faking it one way and throwing it the other way, or double and triple fakes. Each player was put through the drill for one minute, and Billy timed it. The main purpose of the exercise was to increase lateral agility, but it had a secondary effect of improving endurance without having them run those laps which all players dread.

With fielding and hitting as usual in the mix, the practice was a good one. Jamal would be on the mound tomorrow, and so the team liked their chances.

Billy had called Joey, offering him a lift to and from practice. After exchanging a few pleasantries like if Billy found a place to live yet (No) and how work was going for Joey (OK), Billy asked Joey how he was doing in general. Joey went on to reveal that as sorry as he was that Mr. Skinner died, what transpired afterwards was the best thing that could have happened to him. As gut wrenching as it had been, it was also cathartic to get it all out and unburden himself of what had been tearing away at him for so many years. In the aftermath, he enjoyed working with the boys, and of course, reuniting with his two closest friends. He told Billy that he thinks about it every day, but only in a good way. Even his marriage had never been better. They were socializing a lot more, with other couples and dedicating time just for themselves. Billy had seen firsthand how much utter delight Joey had shown in working with the team, and this talk solidified it. From then on, most of their conversations consisted of their two favorite topics- team strategy and reminiscing about the good old days.

Chapter 24

Prior to the Met-Angel game, the earlier contest held lots of implications for the Mets, as the Pirates were squaring off against the Dodgers. Paul, Joey, and Billy were among the interested spectators, and although they knew they controlled their own playoff destiny if they won most or all their remaining games, the trio discussed who they were secretly rooting for.

"Just the sight of that Pirate uniform gets my blood pressure up," said Paul "but, let's think about it this way. Whoever is defeated will have 3 losses and if we can beat that team, we would have the upper hand there. So, probably better if we just act as scouts and spot anything that might be helpful to us down the road." The Pirates prevailed, by a score of 8-5. Pending the outcome of the Met-Angel game, the Mets would either be tied for first with the Pirates, or in a three-way tie for 2nd. Naturally, they hoped for the former.

Before the next game, the guys saw a familiar face carrying a lawn chair, a big smile on his face. It was the one and only Vinnie Panzini. "Hey guys. Vince tells me that you're doing a good job, so I wanted to see for myself. Of course, you do realize that it is taking all three of you to do the job I had done." Back in the day, the kids knew that underneath all that bravado, Vinnie was a great teammate, one that you wanted on your side as he could really get under the opponents' skins. Plus, he could back up his verbal antics with timely hitting.

"Yeah, we're just trying to run with the baton you passed on to us as best as we can, Vinnie," Billy cried out. "How's everything?"

"All is good, Billy. Heard you're still in the market for a house, right? You do know that my wife Camille is a realtor?"

"No, I didn't know that. I'll let Shandra know."

"Hey, Joey. How are you?"

"Good, Vinnie. I'm getting a kick out of helping with the kids here. I have to tell you; Vince is a heck of a player."

"Thanks, Joey, although, like father, like son, I can't imagine he'll be taking the pitcher's mound any time soon, right?"

"That's because, just like you, he is so valuable behind the plate," Billy chimed in.

They all shared a laugh, and then it was time to return to the team.

Hoping to avenge that tough 1-0 loss to the Angels the first time around, the Mets would be sending Jamal Jeffries to the mound, and he again would be matched up with Fred Peters. Peters, with an inning of relief help from Juan Navarro, was brilliant the last time these teams squared off, and on paper it figured to be another close, low scoring contest, with little margin for error on either side.

The home team Mets had their hitting shoes on from the get-go. Jamal tossed a scoreless top of the first, and in the bottom of the inning, Ben, Jamal, and Frankie singled in succession, loading the bases with no one out. With his dad on his feet and leaning against the fence, Vince came through big time, narrowly missing a grand slam as his towering shot went over the head of left fielder Hunter Kurtz for a bases clearing double. Elliot popped up to second and Ron grounded out to first, Vince taking third on the play. With two outs, Ryan came through with a clean single up the middle, and although Jacob's bid for an extra base hit was corralled by Kurtz in left center, the Mets had a 4-0 lead after one inning. Jamal continued to be sharp, and the Mets kept pecking away at Peters and whoever else the Angels threw out there.

When the game was over, with contributions up and down the Met lineup including the bench players, the Mets took the contest by a 10-2 final score. To build up his confidence, they made sure to use Elliot for two innings. Elliot held his own in allowing only one harmless run. In what was shaping up to be an interesting last 3 games, the Mets were now tied with the Pirates for first.

"Hey guys, apparently I'm your good luck charm. You'll see me here some more if I can get away from the restaurant."
"Vinnie, you're still a Springtown legend," Paul chortled, as they made their way to the parking lot.

Chapter 25

The Mets took the next contest in rather easy fashion against the Indians, jumping out in front early, and winning by a 9-3 score. The one-sided affair allowed Paul to play most of the subs for half of the game. The Pirates and Dodgers both won their games as well, against the Reds and the Angels. In what was now all set up to be a thrilling end to the second half of the season, the final week shaped up as follows among the contenders: Saturday - Mets (6-2 record) vs Pirates (also 6-2) and Dodgers (5-3) vs. Reds. Sunday - Mets vs Dodgers and Pirates vs Indians. The Angels, Reds, and Indians were mathematically eliminated from the playoffs, but would be looking to draw gratification by upsetting the contenders, and there was every indication that they would be playing hard.

There were several scenarios involved as far as possible playoff seeding was concerned, including tiebreakers as set up by the league: Should two teams tie for 1st: There would be a one game playoff. The winner would be declared the second half champ, the loser would be awarded second place for the Fall half. In the event of a 3 way tie for 1st (Dodgers winning both of their games, Mets and Pirates each splitting theirs), head to head would be the first tie breaker, then best run differential in all of their second half games, and if necessary run differential among the three teams in just their games against each other. The one to emerge on top would be declared second half champs, the other two in a one game playoff for second.

If there was a clear-cut number one and number two, the league would have to see how they compared to the first and second spots in the first half. If the Pirates and Dodgers prevailed again, in the same order, there would simply be a best two out of three for the championship. If the Mets finished in the top two, there would be playoffs involving all three teams.

As Paul was reviewing this with Billy and Joey at the diner before a Thursday practice, they laughed and threw up their hands in mock surrender, meaning "let's finish in the top two and we'll worry about who we play then."

It was decided that Jamal would go against the Pirates on Saturday. The question was, in a tight game, do they bring in Ryan late in the game if needed, or Elliot? If Ryan, whatever innings he would pitch on Saturday would be deducted from how many he could hurl on Sunday. Since they could not use Jamal on Sunday (assuming he pitched more than three innings), it was decided to hold Ryan for Sunday, since a win against the Dodgers would guarantee no worse than second place for the Mets, no matter what the outcome of the Pirate game.

The other big question was who to start at third base on Saturday: Hank, who had more experience at the hot corner, or the better hitting but not as experienced Ryan. Hank had been improving in the field, and it was decided to go with him for the early innings, then bring in Ryan to get him the requisite number of innings/at bat, and decide then who to finish up at third with depending on how the game was unfolding. They headed to the field for what became a spirited practice heading into a key weekend.

Chapter 26

In the 1960's one of the best NHL goaltenders was Glenn Hall, who reputedly was so nervous, he threw up before every game. In that same decade, before the infamous Super Bowl III, Joe Namath spent a good deal of the preparation week relaxing in a lounge chair by the hotel pool. Some kids at 12 or 13 years old can be no different than adults when it comes to self-awareness. Especially in sports, there are those who are highly cerebral with a tendency to sometimes overthink a situation, or at the very least mentally prepare for situations, and others who "show up", and let the proverbial chips fall where they may. One approach isn't necessarily better than the other. Being tense or being relaxed can both work for someone and against them.

The first 8 games of the second half of the season were, to say the least, interesting for the Met ballclub. After an average first half, they found themselves in a real race to the playoffs, with a completely revamped coaching staff, including a true celebrity guiding them. Attendance for these games was huge, mainly due to the Billy Jeffries factor, effectuating playoff-like atmospheres.

David Dodsworth was certainly a cerebral child, a "thinking man", if you will. Being Paul's son, he too scrutinized statistics, and although he did have a few good moments in a Met uniform, he spent a lot of time on the bench and that gave him lots of time to speculate. As if wise beyond his years, he took an opportunity to give his assessment of their situation with his father. "Dad, I think the one advantage we have going into the last two games, and if we're fortunate, postseason play, is that the overflowing crowds we have had since Mr. Jeffries arrived will better prepare us. What I mean to say is that, we know there will be a lot of people coming to the games this weekend, but we've already experienced that, and it could make our opponents tighter since they are not as used to it. Also, while I believe the Pirates have much more hitting up and down the lineup than us, and the Dodgers have the best overall pitching in the league, Mr. Jeffries and Mr. Harrison have really been drilling us on the fundamentals, and that could make all the difference."

Paul beamed with pride. "Son, I actually think you have something there. I really wish you could have seen Joey and Billy when they were playing. They were not only great in skill, but the moment never got too big for them. I can't vouch for your teammates. Sure, we have a few stars, like Frankie, Vince, and Jamal, but no one can predict how they will react when everything is on the line. This is really the first time they will be playing in a pressure situation. But I like your analogy of being used to large crowds as a plus, and yes, I think you boys have been extremely well coached. As more or less the team's statistician under Vinnie, and from what I had observed, I frankly did not expect us to be vying for first place this year. Of course, the addition of Jamal was immense for us, but I am also seeing a lot of improvement from most of the players. I think we've earned the chance to get into the postseason. I know it's getting late, but how about a game of Stratomatic before you go to bed?"

A winking David replied: "Thought you'd never ask."

Chapter 27

It was an unseasonably cool Saturday morning. The Dodgers and Reds had the early game. As was to be expected, Paul, Billy, and Joey were on hand to check it out, as were some of the Pirate and Met players. The Dodger starting pitchers, Ron Walston and Billy Jones, were both first rate. Dodgers Manager Al Walston opted to go with Jones, and he'd put his son Ron in the following day against the Mets. Walston also knew he could rely on the consistency of Ken Whelan for relief work in either game.

The Dodgers were typically known more for their pitching than batting, but today they had their hitting shoes on, and scorched the Reds starter Howie Klipper from the get-go. With Jones staked to an 8-1 lead after 3 innings, Walston pulled him from the game and inserted Whelan. Although Ron was reluctant to make the change, this was a great tactical move by the Dodger skipper, since he would not only have his son available to pitch as much as all six innings tomorrow, but under league rules could use Jones or Whelan again, each for up to 3 innings. This would give their stellar pitching staff all the ammunition they might need on Sunday. Whelan did his job, limiting the Reds to 2 runs over the final three innings, and with the Dodgers following suit, it resulted in a 10-3 victory for the Dodgers.

After a trip to the snack bar, most of the Dodgers returned to the field to watch their rivals go at it in game 2. The pitching matchup for this game was Frank Carruthers for the Pirates and Jamal Jeffries for the Mets. The Mets were the visitors today. Ben led off with a walk and Jamal followed with a clean single to left. Things were looking up, but Carruthers reared back and struck out the normally clutch Frankie. Vince popped up to short, and Elliot bounced back to the box, and just like that, the promising rally was suddenly over.

Jamal was really bringing it in the bottom of the first, retiring Logan Brockhammer, Bobby Baylor, and Steven Lynch in succession.

Ron, Jacob, and Hank went out in order in the top of the second, and Jamal went back to work. As sharp as he had been in the first inning, suddenly, he had trouble locating in the strike zone, walking the first two batters Rich

Ortega and Alvin Bean. Needing to throw strikes after getting behind in the count on Gerald Linton, he grooved one that Linton jumped on, the ball easily clearing the left field fence for a three-run homer. When Calvin Plunkett followed with a single, Billy called time and trotted out to the mound.

"Hey Jamal, a three-run lead is nothing. We can come back for sure. I know you're not getting your pitches where you want them but concentrate on Vince's target and let's get out of this inning without further damage."

"Okay, Dad."

The talk appeared to pay immediate dividends, as Jamal retired the next two Pirate batters, Hadley Thomas and Ed Lawrence on swinging strikeouts, bringing up the top of the order again. Brockhammer walked, and Baylor plated Plunkett, running hard, with a looping double over the third base bag. With both runners in scoring position and four runs in, Billy paid a second visit to Jamal, with Vince in tow, joining in the discussion. The question was whether to intentionally walk Steven Lynch, setting up a force at any base, including home, and pitch to Rich Ortega, or pitch to Lynch. Left up to a shaken yet proud Jamal, he preferred to pitch to Lynch. Forgetting the macho factor, he liked seeing in his son, Billy knew that loading up the bases would leave them no breathing room and he agreed that this was the right move. Jamal did not have his usual pinpoint control today and could ill afford to groove a pitch to Ortega. Pitching carefully but with a purpose to Lynch, the Pirate number 3 batter took Jamal deep, but Ron made a fine running catch in left center to end the inning without further damage.

In the dugout, Billy conversed with Paul about what to do the rest of the game. It was decided to send Jamal out for the third inning, but if he faltered again, they would take a page out of the Dodgers' playbook they witnessed earlier today and remove him, keeping him in reserve for tomorrow. They also were hoping for their club to cut into the lead.

Lamar, Ben, and Jamal, didn't do them any favors, going out in order. When Jamal gave up 2 more runs in the home half of the third, the decision was made. Elliot would relieve in the fourth. This was not the Mets' day in any way, shape, or form. Carruthers, though not overpowering the rest of the game, was throwing nothing but strikes, and when the Pirates tacked on three more runs against Elliot in the fifth, the only question left was if the Mets could avoid a shutout, which they did when Ryan and Frankie hit back to back doubles in the sixth. Final score: Pirates 9 Mets 1.

How were the coaches going to spin this one towards a deflated and sulking Met team? Billy asked to speak first. "Guys, I am not going to sugar coat this game. We didn't pitch and we didn't hit. In short, we had our butts kicked today. But I have been in enough games in my lifetime to know that baseball can be funny sometimes. I am confident that we will turn it around tomorrow. I would like each of you to go home and put this game in the rear-view mirror as soon as possible. Forget about it. After all, if we win tomorrow, there will be playoff baseball for us in one form or another. Come out on Sunday with a winning attitude; let's erase the slate. Okay? Paul, Joey, anything to add?"

Paul knew to keep it short and to the point, but as was his nature, did want to throw at least one positive out there. "Guys, their 9 runs were all earned. So, no errors of consequence on our part in the field. Ron, great catch on Lynch. Hank, you looked good out there. Vince, you did an excellent job blocking low balls. Hey, Mr. Jeffries speaks from experience. When the game starts tomorrow, the score will be 0-0. He's right - forget the game today and let's be ready to play the Dodgers."

Joey chimed in. "Fellas, it's important never to get down on yourself. The ability to bounce back is what separates a good team from an average team. I have seen enough of you to know you are a good team. So, let's show these Dodgers what we are made of."

Knowing the most expedient way to get the sting of the defeat out of their collective systems, Billy yelled out: "Hot dogs, burgers, and drinks on me." The kids whooped it up as they ran over to the concession stand, jostling for position online. Would the season continue for the Mets after tomorrow, or was Sunday to be their final game? That question would be answered in 24 hours from now.

Chapter 28

On Sunday morning, the Pirates/Indians game was first. Although the Indians engineered some decent scoring off Hadley Thomas, the Pirate hitters made up for it, slugging the Indians' Jack Grant often, winning 10-6. This meant the Pirates won both halves of the season, sporting 8-2 records each time. They would play whichever team emerged as runner up in a best of 3 for the championship and be the home team for game 1 and, if necessary, game 3.

Collectively, the Mets, from coaching staff down to each player, held out little hope of a Pirate loss today, but the early game did have its moments where an upset was possible, and the outcome was closer than predicted. The Mets and Dodgers had identical records at 6-3; the winner would be the second half runner up. If the Dodgers emerged victorious, they, by virtue of coming in second in both halves, would play the Pirates for the title. If the Mets came out on top today, they would be second half runners up, and would play the first half counterpart Dodgers in a best of 3 semifinals, with the winner to play the Pirates for the crown.

As they were warming up, it was difficult to gauge the psyche of the team. They looked alert and ready to go, with a rather intense demeanor, but Billy, Joey, and Paul took that as a good sign. After all, it is always better to be intense than tense. It appeared they had put yesterday's embarrassing loss behind them. Billy pulled Ryan, Jamal, and Elliot aside, informing them they were all eligible to pitch today, Ryan for up to six innings, the others for up to 3. Billy's advice to each of them was simple: Throw with determination for as long as you can and if you falter, there is back up. Last night, Jamal had pleaded with his dad for a chance at redemption by having him be the starting pitcher. Billy was impressed with his son's competitiveness but told him Ryan had earned the right to start this game. He also expressed to Jamal that the team needed to be a united front today, and he fully expected him to support Ryan with some quality chatter from his position at third.

Paul was toying with the idea of starting Hank at third and moving Jamal to right field in place of Lamar but decided to stick with what had gotten them to this point. Substitutions factored into the decision as well, as he had to get Warren, Robert, Denny, and David some innings too.

The coaching staff opted to keep the pre-game pep talk short and sweet. No need to rehash the ramifications of today's game. Rather, there was just a general reminder to back up throws and to get down and block anything in the dirt.

The Mets took the field as Paul, Billy, and Joey each went over to say hello to Vinnie and rub his belly for good luck. Billy waved to his family in the stands, Joey likewise with Kim and the kids, Paul to Becky, and the game was set to begin. The Dodgers knew they were in the postseason one way or another, but preferred to go directly to the championship round, so they were determined. Leadoff batter Ted Kalinsky worked the count full, then smacked a hard grounder to third which Jamal fielded cleanly and threw to Elliot for the first out. Gil Felson popped up to short left field, where a charging Jacob White called off Frankie to make the catch. Tough hitter Dave Willis was next, but Ryan was working the bottom half of the plate beautifully, causing Willis to uppercut his swing, lofting a lazy fly ball to center that Ron Dent caught easily. This was the blueprint the Met brass was hoping for; Ryan throwing strikes, the fielders doing their jobs.

Ron Walston was the ace of the Dodgers deep staff, and when he struck Ben out leading off the bottom of the inning, the Dodgers spiritedly tossed the ball around the infield. Their exuberance was short lived, however. Back to back singles by Jamal and Frankie put runners at the corners. On the first pitch, Frankie took second as Jefferson ignored him. With the count 2-1, Vince's bid for an extra base hit was caught in left center by Willis, but Jamal had alertly tagged up, and scored the game's first run. Elliot then grounded hard but right to Jim Nathan at second for the final out.

The next two innings saw both pitchers completely on their games, neither allowing any scoring. With the start of the fourth inning, both teams made wholesale lineup changes to get the subs their playing time. No one was better than Paul at manipulating the roster; he was able to hold Dennis, a light hitting but excellent second baseman back until the fifth, and as they had done in other games, Warren in for Elliot at first, Robert for Jacob in left, and David in right for Lamar were the bench moves this inning.

Slugger Torrey Jefferson led off for the Dodgers, and he greeted Ryan with a laser blast to right center. David got to the ball on two hops but fumbled it, Jefferson scampering to third. With no outs, Joey motioned for the infielders to position themselves in a few steps. He yelled out to go home if the ball was hit hard enough and to first base if they felt they could not make the play to home in time. It was a solid strategy, but it backfired when Phil Donaldson muscled a pitch into short left for a bloop base hit. Had Frankie been playing at normal depth, he indeed might have caught it, but had no chance from where he was, and just like that, the game was tied at 1. Ryan was still throwing strikes, and on a bouncer back to the mound off the bat of Ron Walston, Ryan pivoted and threw to second for the force play. Ken Whelan and Carl Parks were then retired in rather easy fashion. Billy gave Ryan a high five as he returned to the dugout for hanging tough and limiting the damage.

It would be the subs who helped the cause in the home half of the fourth. The inning appeared to begin without incident when Robert LaChance hit a slow roller to short. The throw from Kalinsky was late, and Robert beat it by a step. "Way to hustle, Robert," screamed an excited Paul from the dugout.

After faking a few bunt attempts that unnerved Walston, David drew a base on balls, putting runners on first and second with no outs. Hank was up now, and the Dodgers were expecting a bunt. He did show bunt as he was taking all the way for a called strike one. That maneuver drew the infielders in at the corners, and though Walston's next pitch had significant velocity which caused Hank to swing late, the batted ball was looped over the head of first baseman Carl Parks. Robert had to hold up to see if the ball was going to be caught, thus each runner was only able to advance one base. Bases loaded now for Jamal, necessitating a trip to the mound for Dodger skipper Al Walston. Flame throwing Ken Whelan was warming up on the sidelines, ready to come in. A strikeout was needed here, so Walston made the change. What a spot for Whelan, who would have to get past Jamal, Frankie, and Vince.

Joey motioned Jamal over for a quick chat while Whelan was finishing his warmup tosses. "I'm pretty sure I know nothing more about this guy than you do, but from where I was standing, I could see him throwing heat. I'll leave it to you if you want to take a strike or not but try not to chase him out of the strike zone."

"Mr. Harrison, my dad will tell you, the harder they throw, the better I hit." Joey couldn't suppress his laugh- that sounded like his friend alright.

Jamal scampered to the batter's box and settled in. The noise was at a feverish level from both dugouts and the bleachers. Jamal looked at one pitch, a ball, then rifled the next serve on a one hop to center. The ball was hit so hard that runners could only move up one base, reloading them, with Robert plating the go ahead run. After making the turn at first and retreating to the bag, Jamal made eye contact with Joey, giving his coach a wink. Frankie was next but Whelan reached back for something extra and struck him out. With one out, Vince was unable to get around on the fastball, and he skied it to second, all runners holding as the umpire shouted out "Infield Fly Rule". Whelan finally ended the Mets' threat by inducing Warren to ground back to the box. Ryan, staked to a 2-1 lead, kept the Dodgers at bay in the fifth, one on a nifty play at second by Dennis O'Brien. In the bottom of the fifth, Whelan also retired the side in order.

It was now the sixth and final inning. Paul put back Jacob in left, and Lamar in right, with Dennis remaining at second. He also kept Warren at first, opting to have Elliot on the sidelines to warm up for a possible relief appearance. Ryan had to face the heart of the Dodger order: Willis, Jefferson, and Donaldson. On a 2-2 pitch, Willis smashed a ball to the right side of the infield, but Dennis made another superb play in the hole and threw to first in time for the first out. Billy took notice of how hard that ball had been hit, but with the lead, decided to let Ryan pitch to Jefferson. Jefferson did not garner his reputation as a big-time hitter for nothing and laced it to left center for a double. Billy called time and trotted out to the mound to talk to Ryan.

"Ryan, you pitched a fantastic game, but I'm going to bring in some help now to get us the win."

Billy had Elliot throwing in the bullpen area but opted for Jamal who he felt would have better control, even though Jamal was not warmed up. Billy realized there were risks involved here - both for the game and reputationally, but he knew the heart of his son better than anyone. Yesterday's dismal outing was eating away at Jamal, and he knew his son was itching for vindication. Hank replaced Jamal at third, Ryan taking a seat between Joey and Paul in the dugout. Jamal completed his warmups and was ready to face Phil Donaldson.

On a 2-1 count, Jamal's pitch was right where he wanted it, but Donaldson was able to fist it between short and third for an infield hit, putting runners at the corners and one out. That brought up Ron Walston. Manager Al Walston wanted to get Donaldson into scoring position and gave him the steal sign, simultaneously giving Ron the take sign to allow the theft of second. Little League teams were programmed not to throw through on a first and third situation because the runner at third would invariably score. Joey, signaling to

Vince, Frankie, and Jamal, thought this was as good a time as any to execute the Cutoff Play, since the Dodgers would not be expecting it. It was a risky move, the biggest being an overthrow by Vince or a poor throw by Frankie, but Joey had faith in his players.

Jamal's first pitch was purposely outside where Vince could handle it easily. As soon as Vince prepared to seemingly throw through to Dennis at second to the shock of the Dodgers, Jefferson, who had been glued to third base, suddenly started for the plate. However, Vince's throw was not all the way to second, but rather to Frankie. Frankie, having prepared himself for this ploy, had already inched forward in from his normal depth to a spot behind the mound and a little to his right, thus positioning himself perfectly to take the throw. The return throw to Vince was a perfect one and nailed a shocked Jefferson who awkwardly tried to slide late. The jubilant Met players went crazy. Joey, Billy, and Paul had to remind everyone, including themselves, that there were only two outs, and a runner still in scoring position at second. But a dejected Ron Walston was no match for a pumped-up Jamal Jeffries, and when a called strike three was uttered by the home plate umpire, the Mets had won the contest 2-1.

The teams lined up for the post game handshakes. Al Walston made his way over to Paul Dodsworth.

"When did you pull that rabbit out of your hat?"

"About 25 years ago, Al. I'm lucky to have coaches who were able to teach it to this group."

"Well, looks like we'll be seeing each other in the playoffs. Good luck. Man, Jamal Jeffries, he looks like the second coming of his father."

"Yeah, and just like his old man was at that age, a great kid all around. Good luck to you too, Al."

The team assembled in the dugout. What a difference 24 hours had made.

Paul stood before the team, "Guys, a total team effort today. Denny, you were tremendous with those plays. Robert, David, the winning rally started with you guys. Ryan, you pitched a heck of a game. Jamal, what a time for you to record your first save. Frankie, Vince - you worked the Cutoff Play to perfection. I would have loved to have taken a picture of Al Walston's face at that moment so you could see it now. His mouth was open so wide, you could have fit a battleship in there. Guys, anything to add?"

Joey jumped to his feet: "The hard work you have all put in paid off today. Yes, we won with some great pitching, but it was the little things that made the difference. I'm proud of each of you. Billy?"

"You were each able to move past yesterday and be in the moment, fully present. That's the true test of resiliency. The games are only going to get tougher from here on in. Mr. Dodsworth will let you know the schedule. Enjoy the win, and the journey ahead."

"Yes, I'll shoot an email to each of you and your parents but if it is like anything in the past, we'll have games Wednesday or Thursday, and one game on the weekend, meaning we'll probably have practice on Tuesday. Snacks on me, boys." As the Mets ran to the snack bar, Vinnie, his voice as loud as though he had been on loudspeaker, bellowed: "What, none of you mention rubbing my "jelly belly" as the real turning point? Seriously, guys, I'd love to be in the dugout with you, but you're all doing a great job with these kids. Billy, I see you reserved a table at Vincente's tonight for six people tonight."

"Yes sir. Kim and Joey, Dodsy and Becky, Shandra and me. Only the best for my best friends."

Chapter 29

At the league meeting the following day it was determined the Mets would be the visiting team in game 1 and if necessary, game 3 because the Dodgers had a better composite season record this year than the Mets (13-7 vs. 12-8). Game 1 would take place on Thursday, game 2 Saturday, and game 3 the following Tuesday. Paul emailed the players and parents that practice would be Tuesday at 6:30 PM. Games 1 and 3 would tip off at 5:30PM, and Game 2 was scheduled for 11AM.

There was a standing rule, since the league was first formed, regarding pitching eligibility for the playoffs. In the regular season, if a player pitched more than 3 innings, he had to wait 72 hours before he could pitch again. In the playoffs, although a pitcher still maxed out at 6 innings per calendar week, he did not have to wait 72 hours to throw again. So, for example, if the player threw 4 innings on Thursday, he could throw up to another 2 on Saturday.

Tuesday's practice was brisk. Joey put the fielders through a vigorous workout and used certain players as base runners to simulate game situations. They also worked on the cutoff play. It would not surprise Dodsy if at Dodger practice, Watson was drilling his team on how to run the basepaths if/when the situation called for it.

"Guys," Joey shouted out to his infielders, "If the runner on first heads for second and Vince fires to Frankie who is in the proper position, but the runner on third doesn't bite and stays put you have one of two options. If Frankie sees there is time to get the runner at second, he could flip it to Ben or Dennis, whomever is playing second in that inning. We must be careful here, though. That could still give the runner on third ample opportunity to then scamper home, assuming that wasn't the third out. Ben and Dennis let's work on your throw home from the second base bag. The other option is for Frankie just to eat it and let the runner take second. My gut feeling is, unless there are two outs, Frankie holds onto the ball. If there are two outs and you see daylight between where the runner is and second base, we try to make the play there. Now, of course, a lot will depend on how speedy the base runners are."

Although the element of surprise had been eliminated against the Dodgers, what Joey liked about this drill was that it kept everyone on their toes, and that's what you want out of a late season practice. Who knows, he thought, maybe if we get to play the Pirates, we can work the play.

Following the fielding drills, Billy threw BP. The kids, who once were completely starstruck by seeing him on the mound, were by now accustomed to it. Billy amped it up a little more than normal to get them ready for the Dodger flame throwers.

Satisfied with the outing, the players were dismissed at 8:00PM. David and Jamal each got a lift home with Ronald, who was there to pick up Lamar. The coaches wanted to stay behind and strategize.

Paul started things off. "Guys, I'm thinking that we don't do too much tinkering with the lineup. We use the formula that got us here." Billy and Joey nodded in agreement. "But we do need to talk about the pitching rotation. Do we go Ryan, Jamal, Ryan, or Jamal in games one and 3?"

Billy wanted to make it clear to them that his answer would be an objective one. "They each have their pluses and minuses. Ryan is always going to be around the plate, and we are not only better defensively with Jamal at third, but we get the bonus of having Ryan's bat in the lineup for the bulk of the game. That said, Jamal is the harder thrower of the two and I feel he can intimidate that Dodger lineup. If we use 3 pitchers in any of the games, I like the idea of going first with speed, then control, then speed, should we pitch Elliot to throw the Dodgers off balance. Starting Jamal twice affords us that opportunity."

Joey was next. "Sometimes, you have to play a hunch and I believe Jamal will be less fazed by a pressure situation. I saw how he handled himself on the mound in relief and also at the plate in the must-win game last week. I know Ryan pitched brilliantly and wields a strong bat, but I'm leaning towards Jamal for game 1, Ryan for game 2."

"Look, we can't go wrong either way. But, think of it like this: If we lose game 1, are we confident in Ryan in game 2 with the whole season on the line?" Paul asked.

"Well you can say the same thing about a possible game 3 if Jamal goes in game 2. I would prefer to take a positive approach and send our best out there in game 1 and put the pressure on the Dodgers. Billy?"

"I'm going to side with Joey. As for any possible damage to Ryan's mindset going into the series, I'll talk with him on Thursday and make it clear that we need him just as badly for a crucial game number 2."

"Okay, we start Jamal in game 1," concluded Paul. "Let me play around with the substitution patterns to get Ryan as many at bats as possible. He's super versatile and we need that flexibility."

"We'll leave that up to you, Dodsy," Joey assured him. "No one is better with the lineup machinations than you."

"I'm feeling good. We are in a really good position with two quality starters at our disposal. Of course, the same can be said about the Dodgers. See you guys Thursday."

Chapter 30

On Wednesday night, Will's team was in a playoff round of their own, and Joey and Kim were front and center to root him on, beaming with pride. Alexa was there too, and she brought along Billy's daughter Jada. The two girls were becoming good friends and were spending a lot of time together as teammates on their youth soccer team.

A neighbor of Joey's, Mitch Simpson, whose son Len played alongside Will, spotted Joey and moved to sit next to him. Simpson held the unofficial title of "neighborhood loudmouth". Although they were always cordial when they would see each other on the block, he was not Joey's cup of tea.

"Hey Joey. Exciting to see our kids in the playoffs, right?"
"Yeah, it sure is, Mitch. Will is super charged up."

"Say, Joey, I've been meaning to ask you. I heard you are coaching with Billy Jeffries and he moved back to Springtown. I know you guys go way back. Must be interesting to say the least."

"It's been very rewarding. It's great to get back out there, and it's a nice bunch of kids to work with."

"Tell the truth, Joey. It must burn you up a little to see Jeffries back here. I mean, you two were great players in High School but only he made it. It must conjure up some bad memories."

Kim, overhearing the conversation, was cringing at the thought of how Joey would handle this. She feared every day since he started coaching again that Joey would crawl back into his shell.

"You know, Mitch, I never once begrudged Billy for getting to that mountaintop and, without going into too much detail, let's just say that I'm in a great headspace since he returned to Springtown. Let's just enjoy the game, ok?"

"Hey, didn't mean to hit a nerve, Joey."

"It's all fine, man. Life is good."

"Sure, great to hear. Guess I'll go rejoin the missus."

Kim stared at Joey, amazed at how he handled the annoying Mitch, and gave his hand a supportive squeeze. She breathed a sigh of relief. Potential catastrophe averted.

"You know, if Simpson had brought that up to me a month ago, I probably would have flown off the handle. But that day with Billy really got me out of the funk I was in. He knows me so well and knew just what I needed to hear. God, it had been such an emotional day. Lou Skinner's funeral, seeing all the guys, it was just so surreal. Billy put things in perspective, and there has been no turning back since then for me."

"Joey, whether it's the games you guys are coaching, the dinner the other night, or just your overall body language, I'm so happy to have the Joey I fell in love with back."

"Hey, you were supposed to marry me for better or for worse," Joey said with a smile on his face.

Kim, wanting to get last licks in, replied: "True, but I'll take the better over the worse any day of the week."

Nothing more needed to be said. They sat back to watch the game. It was a good one for Will as his two hits and a stellar play at shortstop led his team to victory. The car ride home was a happy one, all around.

Chapter 31

On Thursday, time seemed to go by at a snail's pace during school for all the Met and Dodger players. Paul, who primarily worked from home, got up early and interspersed his time working on financial spreadsheets with Met lineup tinkering. He kept mulling the Hank/Ryan substitution pattern over in his mind. How can we get Ryan multiple at bats? Where can we play him? He would discuss this with Joey and Billy at the field.

Parents of the players, especially those that worked outside of the home, did their best to arrange their schedules to make it in time for the start of the game. Joey made sure his last sales meeting of the day was a local one.

At the field, with 45 minutes until game time, Billy pulled Ryan aside for a chat. Ryan was disappointed to hear he wouldn't be getting the ball in game 1 but did not want to show it. He and his teammates took Billy's advice as gospel and knew there was a reason for every decision he and the coaches made. Paul spoke to Ryan next, and promised he would do everything in his power to get Ryan in the game as early as he could, and he should be ready to play either the outfield or the infield, depending on the score and the situation. Also, if Jamal faltered on the mound, he would be the first to relieve him.

The Mets were the visiting team today and would be facing Ron Walston. Walston quickly showed why he had the reputation as an elite pitcher, retiring the side in order on only a dozen pitches. As the Mets took their gloves and ran out to play the field, Billy advised Joey and Dodsy that when the team came back in, he was going to tell them to step out of the box every once in a while to try to upset Walters' rhythm, as the Dodger ace seemed to be in real groove. Jamal, throwing hard and with confidence, retired the Dodgers, giving up only a walk with one out to Gil Felson. And so, it went for three innings; both pitchers were practically unhittable. Base runners were few and far between, neither team so much as placing a runner in scoring position.

In the top half of the fourth, Frankie fisted a ball through the left side of the infield and took a big turnaround first. When substitute left fielder

Rick Smithers bobbled the ball, Frankie headed for second, and slid in safely, avoiding Jim Nathan's sweeping tag attempt. With Vinnie cheering his namesake on from beyond the fence along the first base side, Vince worked the count in his favor, and on a 3-1 pitch, he tattooed Walters' serve over the left field fence for a 2-run homer. As soon as Vince crossed home plate, mobbed by his teammates, Al Walters sprinted out to the mound. It took a lot for Al to control his emotions and not to rag on his son for grooving one to Panzini with first base open, but Ron got the message, nonetheless. He then made quick work of Elliot and Ron Dent, fanning both. Ryan was up next, having taken over for Jacob in the batting order, and, heeding Billy's plea to step out of the box after each pitch to slow Walters down, Ryan reached out on an outside pitch and stroked it to right for a base hit. From the coaching box at first, Billy high fived Ryan when time was called. That brought up Robert LaChance, in for Hank now. Robert was unable to get around on any of Walters' pitches, and struck out, leaving Ryan stranded.

Al Walters was still heated about the pitch selection to Vince and motioned his son over to the end of the dugout bench. Coaching your own offspring was never easy. It was important to be fair, objective, and critical when warranted but it was a fine line. If you went too far, it could destroy your child at an impressionable age. Al Walters was by no means a tyrant, though, and one look into Ron's eyes told him the boy had already gotten the message, so he simply put his arm around him. No words were exchanged or necessary during this silent pep talk.

Meanwhile, in the Met dugout Paul reviewed his substitution printout, and the team settled in for the moment as Jamal prepared to face the heart of the Dodger order. Dave Willis, Dodger number 3 hitter, led off and with a ball to right field that Ryan got a late jump on, Willis stopping at first. Cleanup batter Torrey Jefferson, owning a game winning home run against the Mets in an earlier game, helped his team's cause with a one hopper over the mound and into center for a single, putting runners at first and second. With Phil Donaldson up, Jamal, perhaps overthrowing, uncorked a wild pitch, both runners advancing. Joey shouted out to his infielders that with a two-run lead, the play was to first base. It being the fourth inning, Billy huddled up with Paul and Joey and decided to pitch to Ron Walston rather than walk him, especially since there were no outs. Billy thought about paying a visit to the mound but opted to let Jamal work out of this on his own. Even without a mound trip, Jamal could not dismiss his dad's yelling out from the top of the dugout to concentrate on the batter.

Walston was of course looking to make up for the runs he had given up, and he swung extra hard on Jamal's pitches. He missed the first two, but not the third one. With his dad shouting out to ease up on the swing a tad, he sent a two-strike pitch deep to center field. Ron Dent had no time to get his glove on the screaming liner that sailed over his head and did everything he could in pursuit to keep Walston from advancing too far. The speedy center fielder's throw to Robert at third would have nailed Walston had he not listened to his dad exhorting him to hold up at second. It was a nice play by Dent, but the damage had been done. Just like that, the game was tied up, with Jamal in trouble.

This time, Billy paid a visit to the mound. Jamal was usually even-tempered, but now he appeared rattled. Billy saw immediately that he needed to settle him down, and the best way to do that was to focus on the task at hand, not what had already occurred.

"Jamal, we need to keep Walston from scoring. Concentrate on the hitters. Got it?"

"Got it."

Billy didn't see the need to tell his son that this was the tail end of the batting order now up for the Dodgers, with substitutes. That could often cause a pitcher to lose concentration and miss the target.

Joey yelled out to Hank and Frankie to do what they could to hold the runner, Walston, on a grounder to them. Whether Jamal knew who he was facing or not, he was able to focus, and worked out of the tough jam without Walston scoring. He got three successive outs, the first two by fanning the batters, the last on an easy grounder back to the box.

Lamar, back in, led off the fifth and after fouling off several two strike pitches, worked out a base on balls. Paul had a tough choice to make. Did he bring back Ben, or let Dennis hit? Ben had the superior bat, Dennis the steadier glove. Since both had played the requisite two innings and had each had at least one plate appearance, Paul decided to take advantage of the free substitution rule and opted to let Ben hit. The situation screamed for a sacrifice to get the speedy Lamar into scoring position. Joey did flash the bunt sign to Ben, but Walters' first pitch bounced in the dirt. When Jefferson could not come up with it cleanly, Lamar took off for second and slid in safely.

Felson was now playing third and Parks was at first, and both were creeping in. Expecting the diminutive Ben to still bunt, Joey flashed the hit sign. It was all Felson could do to get his glove on the hard grounder off Ben's bat, the ball ricocheting towards shortstop. Kalinsky had no play, and Lamar advanced to third. With runners on the corners, Joey gave Ben the steal sign. Paul had to chuckle and said to the players in the dugout: "Wouldn't it be nuts if Al Walston stole our Cutoff Play move?"

Billy whispered to Ben to get in a run down if a throw was made, to afford Lamar the opportunity to score. Jamal got the take sign, and Jefferson simply tossed the ball back to the mound, Ben taking second. Al Walston called time to pay a mound visit. After making sure Ron was up to the task of pitching to the heart of the Met order, the discussion centered around walking Jamal to create a force at any base. It was decided to pitch to him, but very carefully, and for sure, not to groove anything.

Jamal was normally a cool cucumber, but playoff baseball can unnerve the best of them, and he uncharacteristically swung at a pitch out of the strike zone, sending a pop up to first. Parks made the catch and the runners had to hold up. One out. Frankie fought off a tough two strike pitch, but could only one hop it to the mound, where Walston fielded the ball and fired it to home and Jefferson put the tag on Lamar. Two outs now. With Vince up, no amount of belly rubbing on his dad for good luck would be enough this time. He skied it to left and into the glove of Phil Donaldson for out number 3.

Incredibly, the Mets did not score with two runners in scoring position, three chances, and with their best hitters up. Billy and Joey reminded the team to not get down on themselves as they went out into the field for the bottom of the fifth. Billy especially knew that this was easier said than done even with professionals, let alone impressionable kids, and that included his 12-year-old son, so Billy spoke briefly to Jamal before having him go out there.

Jamal would face the top of the Dodger order, starting with Ted Kalinsky. He was not your prototypical leadoff batter, in that he seldom drew walks, but he did hit for a high average. Kalinsky hit it hard, but it was a two hopper to Frankie who threw him out by three steps. Gil Felson swung through a high hard pitch, fanning for out number 2. Dave Willis was not going to go down as easily, but his bid for a hit on a smash between first and second was gobbled up by Dennis on one hop, who tossed to first for the third out.

As the Mets returned to the dugout in a happier frame of mind, they noticed the Dodgers made a pitching change. Ken Whelan was in. He would be facing Elliot, Ron, and Jacob. Joey knew from experience that although Whelan threw hard, he was usually around the plate, so there would be no take signs. He wanted the guys to go up there swinging at the first good pitch. Elliot was unable to get the sweet part of the bat on the ball, and although he skied it, the lazy fly ball was an easy catch in center by Willis. Ron grounded out, short to first for out number two. Jacob had a nice at bat, and although he didn't quite get around on Whelan's serves, he sliced a seeing eye hit into right. However, he and the Mets could go no further, as Ryan grounded out to second.

As the Mets took the field in the bottom of the sixth, Billy stopped Jamal, just to make sure he was in a good head space. Assuring his dad, he was fine, he went out to throw warm up tosses. Back to back to back sluggers supreme awaited Jamal: Torrey Jefferson, Phil Donaldson, Ron Walston. Jamal was in his last inning of work today and he left nothing in the tank, blowing fast ball after fast ball past the batters. Jefferson could only muster a foul tip, strike three into Vince's glove. Donaldson took a called third strike, and although Walston made contact with two strikes, it was a tapper right in front of the plate that Vince grabbed and threw to first for the third out. Onto extra innings they went.

Whelan disposed of Hank, Lamar, and Dennis rather easily. Faced with having to relieve Jamal on the mound, the Met coaches opted to bring in Elliot. The bottom of the Dodger lineup was due up and they didn't want to take any chances. Elliot's heat however was no match for the Dodgers. Although he went to three balls on two of the hitters, the side was retired in order.

Convinced that Whelan could go a third inning, something he was not accustomed to in the regular season, Dodger skipper Walston sent him out to face 2,3, and 4 in the Met lineup. Jamal started the inning off with a line drive that was caught by Kalinsky at shortstop. Frankie followed with a base hit to center but was left stranded by Vince and Elliot.

Elliot completed his warmups and was set to face the top of the order. Kalinsky grounded out to Jamal, now playing third base, but then Elliot had trouble finding the plate, walking Felson on four straight pitches out of the strike zone. Billy had Ryan warming up on the sideline, and, not liking what he just saw with Elliot, contemplated making a pitching change. Paul did make Billy aware that having Ryan pitch in this spot would reduce his innings eligibility for game 2, and without Jamal available, it meant they would have to use Elliot again for at least an inning, or more if Ryan got out of this jam and was to pitch more innings. "That's a good point, Dodsy. Okay, let me go out there and try to settle Elliot down."

Billy's talk did help Elliot refocus on the strike zone, and he retired Willis on a fly to Ron in center. That brought up Torrey Jefferson, owner of a game winning homer vs. Elliot already this season. Jefferson calmly took a called strike one, a beauty over the outside corner. Working the count to 2-1, he found a pitch right in his wheelhouse, sending it on a line in the gap between Jacob and Ron, where neither could cut it off, the ball rolling towards the outfield fence. With Felson racing at full speed, Ron fired it to Frankie, who wheeled and threw home, but not in time, Felson sliding across the plate before Vince could apply the tag. The Dodgers alternatively created mob scenes around Felson and Jefferson, as the dejected Mets slowly made their way to the bench.

In the dugout, the coaches wanted to say something inspiring, and this time, it was Joey who got it going. "Guys, okay, tough loss, but this is the playoffs, and nothing is going to come easy. I liked the way we battled today. Maybe we didn't have the timely hitting we needed, but I cannot think of a single thing we did wrong out there. We're going to go out there on Saturday and give it our all."

Billy wanted to speak to Elliot one on one, so he kept his comments to the team general in nature. "Think of it this way; you already beat the Dodgers in an elimination game last week, to get to the playoffs. You played well with your backs up against the wall, so let's just do it again. Paul, anything else you'd like to add?"

"Just keep in mind some of you may be asked to play in positions you are not used to, so each of you need to be ready at any time. Game 2 is at 11AM, so let's make sure we are all here by 10:15."

Billy saw the looks of frustration on the boys. He tried a different approach. "Hey, this is supposed to be fun. There is nothing better than performing against stiff competition and standing toe to toe with them. That is what I saw today, and frankly, what I have seen from each of you from first practice and throughout the season. It's one game, one loss. We'll bounce back on Saturday; I'm sure of it. See you then."

As the 3 coaches left together for their cars, Billy sighed, "Nearly 3 decades later, and some things just never change - If we're going to win, we'll have to do it the hard way."

"I just don't want the season to end yet; I'm having too much fun," said Dodsy. He and Joey walked away, with a wave and a smile.

Chapter 32

Some teams play better under pressure while others fall apart. Some teams have a killer instinct to finish off their opponent, while others, perhaps subconsciously, take their foot off the gas pedal too easily. Lou Skinner's teams always used to project a workman-like approach, emblematic not only of their skipper, but due to the players themselves, notably Paul's two coaches. How he prayed that some of that outlook would shift to the current group.

As the Mets assembled Saturday morning, Paul Dodsworth's immediate task was to gauge the team's aggregate psyche. This would help him formulate his pregame speech. If today's game was to be like the other Dodger battles, it figured to be close and low scoring. With Ryan pitching, it saved Paul the job of trying to figure out how to get him multiple at bats. With Jamal at third and Jacob and Lamar starting in the corner outfield spots, it projected a strong defense for most of the contest. Sure, Dennis was the better glove at second, but Ben was not exactly a slouch. Ben was also showing his strength lately by getting on base and setting the table.

Joey and Billy liked the body language during warmups; if they were to be successful today, it would come down to executing. The Mets were the home team today, and after Paul gave out the lineup and batting order, he reminded the guys to remember what his coaches had been preaching all along - stay alert, back up and/or line up throws, and remain even keeled no matter what the score was.

Ryan, as usual, was throwing strikes to start off the first, getting ahead of the batters. But with two outs in the top of the first, Dave Willis took Ryan deep. His fly ball, perhaps aided a bit by the wind, sailed over the left field fence. Just like that, the Dodgers were out in front. After Torrey Jefferson grounded out to Frankie, the Mets came in from the field and prepared to face Billy Jones.

Jones, like Ryan, was a strike throwing machine, though he displayed better velocity. But, it was a determined Met club that he faced, and on consecutive singles by Ben and Jamal, it brought up Frankie Martinez, who delivered big time, hammering Jones' first pitch just inside the third base line for a double that scored both runners. Vince's bid for a base hit was taken away on a pretty play by Jim Nathan at second, Frankie advancing to third. With Elliot up, Jones uncharacteristically uncorked a wild pitch that bounced past Jefferson, then took a 45-degree angle off the back stop. Frankie, aggressive at third, saw the play develop in front of him, and raced home, scoring well ahead of Jefferson's throw to the covering Jones, for the third run. Elliot popped up to short for the second out. Ron put good wood on one, but it was caught in centerfield, retiring the side.

The Met dugout was pumped up as Ryan returned to the hill nursing a 3-1 lead. Manager Walston's strategy was for his players, especially the bottom of the order, to take a strike, knowing that Ryan Bernstein's two strike pitch would be no faster than any of his other pitches, and Walston's hope was that Ryan would miss the plate here and there, resulting in walks. But Ryan was his typical self on this day and walks, or even three ball counts, were far and few between. While he breezed through the next three innings, the Mets' bats were alive, and when relatively light hitting Warren Cameron, Robert LaChance, and David Dodsworth singled consecutively in the home half of the fourth, it proved to be the catalyst for a huge inning. When the dust had cleared, the Mets had plated another five runs, and took a commanding 8-2 lead into the fifth. Billy and Paul mulled over removing Ryan now, but decided to send him out there for at least the fifth inning. Ryan, continuing to emulate an Iron Mike Machine, was hitting Vince's target consistently, and although he gave up another run on back to back doubles by Jefferson and Donaldson, he survived any further damage.

With Ken Whelan on in relief of Jones, Vince and Elliot got that run back with their own back to back doubles, and Ron drove in Elliot with a clean base hit to left center. Whelan got the next three outs, and although Ryan would be eligible to pitch as long as possible on Tuesday (it being a new week and 72 hours later), with a 7 run lead it was decided to give Elliot some mound work. Elliot looked sharp, retiring the Dodgers in order. In what few could have predicted based on past games, the Mets breezed to a 10-3 win to even up the best of three series.

In the aftermath of this blowout win, Paul, Billy, and Joey opted to play it down, and disregarding the outburst of runs scored today, called for a Monday night practice at the local Indoor Batting Cages, just to keep the kids sharp and focused. Tuesday's game, a 5:30PM start, would allow both teams to use each and any of their 3 pitchers for as long as needed, with one caveat: Game

91

1 of the Championship round vs. the Pirates was tentatively set to start the same week, on Saturday, which meant for the surviving team that the number of innings availability per pitcher would be lessened by how many innings he threw on Tuesday.

It didn't take Paul, Billy, and Joey very long to come up with a pitching game plan. On a Sunday night conference call, they each agreed to worry only about the deciding game against the Dodgers and stick to the strategy they had mapped out: Jamal to start, followed if need be by Ryan, and then Elliot. No sense in worrying about the Pirates; if they didn't beat the Dodgers, there was no next game.

Chapter 33

During his playing career, Billy was besieged with requests for interviews across all forms of media - television, radio, podcasts, newspapers, and magazines. Interviewers found him articulate, insightful, and affable. So, when his agent called him, not long after his move back to Springtown, with the news that Sports Illustrated wanted to do a feature on him, he wasn't surprised. He knew from the crowds in the stands in Springtown and all of the cameras, that word of his Little League coaching had spread. The interview was to take place on Monday, the day before the deciding game against the Dodgers. They arranged to meet at Billy's parents' home where Billy, Shandra, and the kids were still residing, then drive over to the ballfield for the remainder of the interview.

Billy had one demand before agreeing to be interviewed-- the article would not be published until after the Little League season was over. In true Billy Jeffries fashion, he did not want to take anything away from the playoffs. SI agreed. The angle of the feature would be a retired ballplayer, a great one at that, giving back to the community in a place where it all had begun. Billy wanted to be respectful of the names he'd likely bring up in the interview, especially the Skinner family, whom he knew valued their privacy. He placed a call to Lisa Skinner.

"Hi Mrs. Skinner. It's Billy Jeffries."

"Billy, how wonderful to hear from you. I understand that you've moved back to Springtown. That is amazing."

"Yes, we're living with my folks until we find a place."

"Your parents must be so happy, Billy."

"They are. Plus, my wife's parents live in Jersey, so it's good all around."

"Billy, I can't thank you enough for coming to pay your respects to Lou. It meant a lot to me and my family. You know, he coached for several years before taking over and running the league, but I do believe that the best time he ever had was coaching your team."

"Well, Mrs. Skinner......."

"Please, Billy, call me Lisa."

"Er, okay, Lisa. I owe a lot to coach Skinner. He was a wonderful person."

"He was that, Billy. Still can't believe he's gone."

"I know, Lisa. I am happy we are getting this chance to speak. I wanted to run something by you. Sports Illustrated wants to do an interview with me, and I was wondering if it would be okay with you if I mention Mr. Skinner, and his influence on me."

Lisa did her best to suppress crying out as tears streamed down her face, and she replied: "Oh Billy, Lou would have loved that. Not so much the notoriety, but that you still felt that way about him. So, you go right ahead and feel free to express whatever you want. Now I have a request for you. I want you to pick a date so I can have your family, including your parents, over for dinner. Promise me you'll talk it over with them and get back to me?"

"Deal. You'll hear from me, soon. Stay well, Lisa, and again, thanks. It was great talking to you."

"Likewise, Billy. Thank you! Goodbye."

When the SI crew showed up at the Jeffries' home, they positioned Billy and Shandra next to each other on the family room couch. The interviewer went through a barrage of questions, wanting to get to the crux of what made a famous person like Billy Jeffries decide to return to Springtown and coach Little League. There was no way Billy was going to bring up his intervention with Joey; that wasn't something to be shared with the world.

"I was living in Ann Arbor when I received a phone call from my cousin Ronald that Lou Skinner, my former Little League coach, suddenly died. Mr. Skinner meant so much to me when I played for him in my youth, I really cannot adequately put it into words. I just knew without hesitation that I needed to pay my respects to his family and attend the funeral. When I got here, I was pleasantly surprised to see several of my ex-teammates, including some who were also living away from here, had come for the funeral too. In addition, it gave me the opportunity to reconnect with two of my closest childhood friends,

Joey Harrison and Paul Dodsworth, both of whom still live in Springtown. On the night following the funeral, we all met for dinner. He'll kill me if I don't give him a shout out - Vinnie Panzini, my ex-teammate, owns Vincente's, the best restaurant in town and that's where we ate. Really excellent food, by the way. You should try it while you're in town, that is if you can get a reservation, and yes, feel free to mention my name. Anyway, I realized that as great as Ann Arbor was for my family and me, there's no place like home. My family is here, as are my roots. As good fortune would have it, Paul had just taken over managing a Little League team, and after conferring with Joey, we thought it would be fantastic for the three of us to coach together, not only to further honor the memory of Lou Skinner, but frankly, that it would be a fun thing to do."

The interviewer who had obviously done his homework retorted: "You mention Joey Harrison. We did some checking. Seems he went to UCLA on a sports scholarship, but never made it past college, right?"

Billy was kicking himself for having brought Joey's name up; it could have serious consequences if the reporter misrepresented anything that he said. Glancing at his watch and stalling for time to construct just the right answer, he suggested they head over to the field. "I'd really like for you to see where it all began for me, so why don't we head out to the field, and we can continue this there? You can follow Shandra and me in your car, okay?"

As soon as they got into their car, Billy smacked the steering wheel. "Why did I have to bring up Joey's name? That wasn't how I wanted the conversation to go."

"Billy, come on, you heard them say they had done their homework. They would have brought it up anyway."

"Do you think I should call Joey now?"

"No. You didn't say anything negative about him. It's not like it's going to be in tomorrow's newspaper. Answer their questions and tell Joey in person that the interviewer asked about him and his career. I always find that tough conversations amongst friends should happen face to face. And I think Joey will be fine."

"You're right. I'll figure it out. I'll tell the truth and hopefully my admiration for Joey will come through in the article. I shouldn't censor myself based on

Joey's psyche. The reporter will interpret my words however he chooses to. That I can't control."

Billy parked next to the SI crew and together they walked towards the field, leading them directly to the well-manicured mound. Billy wanted to get Joey's portion of his story out of the way as fast as possible, with little room for vacillating dialogue. "Circling back to your last question on Joey Harrison. The answer is simple: He had a serious leg injury at UCLA and could no longer play at the elite level. End of story. So, here we are, standing on the exact mound where I once pitched. If someone told me then that not only would I be lucky enough to make it to the big leagues, but it would be as a pitcher and not a hitter, now, that's a storyline I would have never believed."

As best he could, Billy went on to share some of the highlights of their Little League championship season. Noting that the angle they wanted to keep exploring was his return to the place where it all started, he talked about the present: the three coaches trying their best to emulate Lou Skinner, the unbelievable feeling of coaching his son on the same ballfield where his love for the game began, the warm welcome and respect he received from everyone in Springtown, and in general, how coaching has solved the issue of withdrawal from playing.

Mutually satisfied with how the interview went, and after plenty of photos were taken (Billy on the mound, Billy in centerfield, Billy in the dugout), they said their goodbyes. Shandra reminded Billy that there was a house that just opened on the market that they needed to see this afternoon. He asked that he drop her back at home, and that they go in separate cars, so he could leave directly for the batting cages. He also put in a call to Dodsy, asking him if he could pick up Jamal and bring him. Billy and Shandra met up with Camille Panzini at the house, loved what they saw, both feeling that this could be the one. Everything was falling into place.

Chapter 34

The coaches felt the batting cage "practice" was a mere tune-up for tomorrow night's game, something a little different to keep the boys from any possible ennui. With one eye on the players as they took their turns in the batting cage, Billy told Joey that he had been interviewed by Sports Illustrated earlier today.

"Yeah, they wanted to feature an old man like me coming back home to his roots in Springtown. It was pretty basic stuff, but always fun to relive some of the past playing under Lou Skinner."

"Wow, SI- who would have ever thought?" Joey shook his head and gazed in the distance.

"We talked about us, the three childhood friends, together again, coaching this team. They did ask about you, specifically."

Joey was taken aback. "What did they want to know about me?"

"Well, they knew you had gone to UCLA and they asked what I knew about that."

Billy did not want to make a big deal of it, but he felt like these conversations with Joey were always tenuous.

"I just told them you hurt your leg badly, and that was it."

Joey stared at Billy, for what seemed like a few beats too long. He took a deep breath for effect, then put his arm around Billy, laughed and said: "Billy- this is awesome. A huge deal, I couldn't be happier for you. And hey, sounds like there's a chance I'll get to see my name in SI too now. Life is good." Billy exhaled a massive sigh of relief. He added that he couldn't be sure what would make the actual article, but the interviewer did love the camaraderie among the three longtime friends. Shandra was right, as usual.

Each kid hit three rounds, then made a visit to the snack bar. The three coaches agreed to meet up at the diner for coffee at 4:00PM tomorrow to go over last-minute strategy.

Later that evening, David Dodsworth, having finished his homework, came downstairs.

"Hey, Dad. What's good on TV tonight?"

"Game of Thrones is on in a half hour. What's up?"

"Dad, speaking for all the guys on the team, win or lose tomorrow, it's been so awesome and fun since you guys took over. I mean, Mr. Panzini was great too, don't get me wrong and he had us cracking up, even in games. But to tell you the truth, I never thought the team would get this far. Laughing is one thing but winning is the best feeling."

"I'm really glad to hear you say that. I know being in the presence of a celebrity like Billy Jeffries has been super exciting for everyone, me included. Plus, you are getting the absolute best of instruction. Adding Jamal to the roster was huge for us too. You know, David, I never got the chance to play when I was your age. Sure, the guys and Mr. Skinner treated me with respect, but I would have loved to have been in on the action. I'm proud of you, son. I know it's not easy getting limited playing time, but you've been a great sport and a team player."

"I don't mind, Dad. I know I'm far from the best player. I did want to ask you - How good was Billy Jeffries as a kid? I mean, did you ever think he would become so great and so famous?"

"Billy was always a tremendous player, the best on our team from day 1. He was fearless at the plate and came up with so many big hits, plus, man oh man, could he ever play the center field position. He had such incredible instinct, and as you can imagine, a gun for an arm. Don't forget, he carried those skills onto the playing field in high school. I'm not certain if I would have pegged him as a big time closer, but, yeah, he was destined for greatness"

"And Mr. Harrison?"

"Joey was great too. A terrific all-around player. He batted second for us, and maybe he didn't have the power numbers that Billy or our third baseman

Ike Eichorn had, but he came through with his share of gap hits and he made all the plays at short, routine ones as well as spectacular ones. When he got to high school, he shot up in height and weight, and was able to display more power. But, you know, David, as great as these guys were on the field, they were even better off it. I'm sure you can see that, even now."

"Yeah, they are so cool and down to earth about everything, Dad. Mr. Jeffries especially is so nice to everyone who comes up to him. I think I'd become annoyed if I were him, having to take pictures and sign autographs every minute, but he seems so cool with everything."

"He just wants to feel normal and to be treated like everybody else. After all, the last time he lived here, he wasn't the superstar he is today. I think he's done a bang-up job."

"For sure, Dad. Want me to get mom for you so you can watch the show?"

"Why don't you watch it with us?", asked Paul.

"Dad, c'mon. I'm 12. I'm going to play a little Madden Football and go to bed."

Paul smiled, tousled David's hair, and shifted the easy chair into the lounge position. He loved Game of Thrones and would try not to get too distracted with tomorrow's lineup in his head.

Chapter 35

The Met brain trust ordered coffees and danishes in a virtually empty diner due to the off-hour. From the outset of the season, they never wavered-Dodsy would have full control of the lineup and substitutions, unless he asked for their help. Today, however, was one of those times.

Paul seemed visibly more anxious than usual. "I know that our bats came alive last game, but I think our strategy should be to plan for a tight ballgame and try to maximize our defensive alignment. So, where is the strength at the positions we normally sub in and out of? Second base - Do we continue to reserve Dennis for the late innings, when Ben's been wielding such a hot bat? Third base - We'll start Hank, but do we sub Ryan in for him, or at other positions? As for the outfield, I would want to start and end the game with Jacob in left and Lamar in right, like we have been doing. Even though it's unlikely, we must prepare for a subpar game on the mound by Jamal, and where in the field do I put him if need be?"

Billy leaned in. "It's all going to depend on the score. If Jamal must be removed from the pitcher's spot, it will depend on what inning we're in. My vote is we get Ryan in the field as early as possible, maybe even the 3rd inning, and since you need to find a position for Warren for a few innings, have Ryan play third and Warren play first. That means Robert and David at the corner outfield spots for a few innings. As for Dennis, I would plan on playing him in the fourth and fifth innings, and if we need a late plate appearance for Ben, I think you can weigh the pros and cons based on the score at the time. Dodsy, please don't take this the wrong way because I know how much you care, but you have done such a superb job of running the team, so my best advice is not to overthink this. Just rely on a combo of your instincts and how the game is unfolding."

Joey chimed in. "I know, heck we all know, that we would love to get to the championship round. You've poured over the team stats as if you were studying for a final exam. You've done the groundwork. The preparedness is there; let it play out. We have faith in you."

"Guys, you're the best. I always marveled at how calm you both are in pressure situations between the lines. I don't have it in me, I guess. You are so right, Joey. Getting to the finals would be amazing, and back when I took over the team, I never thought it would be possible. Don't worry, I'll take my cues from you once we get to the field and go with the flow. I'll be cool as a cucumber. I don't want any of the boys getting uptight on my account."

It was 4:40 when they left the diner. The deciding semi-final contest was just about 45 minutes away. One team would advance to play the formidable Pirates for the title. Would it be the Mets, or the Dodgers?

Chapter 36

The opposing starting pitchers, Jamal Jeffries and Ron Walston, each completed their warmup sessions. Billy took stock and noted that Jamal seemed revved up for the game yet in control of his emotions, which is what one wants to see in a do-or-die situation like this one. There's a fine line between being keyed up and being anxious. The latter could lead to a lack of concentration and overthrowing. In the opposing dugout, no doubt Dodger manager Al Walston was looking for the same in his son. Billy told Jamal not to hold anything back. Both Ryan and Elliot would be available to pitch in relief if need be. Same with the Dodgers, who had Billy James and Ken Whelan waiting in the wings.

Dodsy's pregame speech was short and sweet, merely reminding the players to back up throws, keep their heads in the game regardless of the score, and echoing what Joey had been telling them from day one: always be on alert as though the ball is going to be hit to you.

Paul and Al met at home plate with the 2 umpires who would be calling the game to review the ground rules. The managers shook hands and wished each other good luck. There was an overflow crowd on hand, including Pirate skipper Dan Murchinson and many of his players. The Dodgers took the field and Ron Walston trotted out to the mound to begin his warmup tosses to Torrey Jefferson.

Ben Caloway stepped into the batter's box, and the ump's cry of "Play Ball" was bellowed at a decibel that belied the enormity of the game. Ben worked the count full, fouling off a few two strike pitches, but ultimately Walston got the better of him, inducing a tap back to the box. Jamal wasted no time and jumped on the first pitch he saw, hammering it over Ted Kalinsky's head at shortstop for the game's first hit. Frankie Martinez helped the Met cause when he placed an outside fastball between first and second and into right field, Jamal scampering all the way to third. That brought up Vince Panzini, and in turn it brought his parents Vinnie and Camille out of their chairs along the first base side. Although Vinnie had been banned from the actual playing field, that didn't stop him from rooting his son on from his spot. "Let's go Vince, show them what you're made of."

Knowing Jamal's speed, Al Walston had his infield playing back, conceding the run. After Frankie stole second on the first pitch, Watson shouted out that the play for the outfielders was to throw to third to keep Frankie from advancing. On a 2-1 pitch, Vince lofted a fly ball to deep left. Inexplicably ignoring his manager's instruction, Ken Whelan caught it with his strong arm and fired to Jefferson, as he thought he had a play at the plate. Prior to the at bat, Joey had whispered to Jamal to run hard no matter what. Although Whelan's throw was strong, it was slightly offline and not in time. Jefferson reached for the ball and then dove to try and apply the tag on Jamal, but the speedy Jamal scored. Frankie was on high alert and seeing the play at home in front of him, took off for third, beating Jefferson's throw. Al Walston, known for his temper, was furious with Whelan for not listening to him. He would have a talk with him when the top of the inning was over.

Elliot Markow was up next, and Ron Walston threw a beauty of a two-strike pitch for a huge strikeout. But Ron Dent came through big time, his hard grounder up the middle reaching the outfield. Frankie scored easily. The inning ended with Jacob White grounding out to first, Carl Parks making the play unassisted.

Ted Kalinsky led off for the Dodgers, and he was disposed of easily by Jamal through the strike out route. Gil Felson followed with a soft grounder that Ben gobbled up and threw to first; it was looking good for Jamal. However, Dave Willis was not going to be denied, and his rising shot to left field cleared the fence for a home run. As the umpire threw the ball back into play, Jamal glanced at the dugout and his dad gave him the palms down sign, meaning be cool and don't let the one run get to him. Jefferson stepped in, and he got into it a little with Vince.

"Brand new ballgame, Panzini."

"Not quite, dude, or can't you count? The score is 2-1."

"Not for long, my friend."

"We'll see about that." Now directing his chatter to his battery mate, he shouted, "C'mon Jamal. Let's get this stiff."

Although it was still early in the game, this was a classic confrontation of top pitcher versus stud hitter. On a 2-1 pitch, Jefferson sent it deep to left, but it was foul by several feet. Jefferson ran the count full and then fought off a tough pitch on the inner half of the plate, grounding it in the hole to Frankie's left. Frankie had been shading Jefferson to pull, and therefore had to go far to his left to snare the ball. He balanced himself using his glove along the dirt as leverage and threw to Elliot in time for the third out. As the Mets ran off the field, high fiving Frankie, Paul Dodsworth glanced at Joey and thought to himself, hmmm, where have I seen such good shortstop play before?

For the next few innings, both pitchers settled into the game, and the score remained 2-1 Mets heading into the fifth inning. Jacob reached out and poked a single into the hole between short and third. Hank Neilson laid down a perfect bunt, was thrown out at first, as Jacob slid safely into second. David Dodsworth was next, and he gave the Mets bench and their supporters a thrill by lining one over first before it hooked foul. Good try, but it was all for naught, as David struck out. That brought up Dennis, and he too struck out.

Jamal strode out to the mound, six outs away from delivering a huge victory. He would be facing the bottom of the Dodger order. Ken Whelan was up first, and he sent a hard grounder to third. Hank, back in there, fielded it cleanly and fired it to Elliot for the first out. Carl Parks was a strikeout victim for out number two. Jim Nathan worked the count in his favor at 3-0, but Jamal got the next two over to Nathan, who had been taking all the way. On a full count, Jamal blew the next one by him, ending the fifth inning in fashion.

In the dugout as the Mets prepared to bat in the top of the sixth, Paul urged his team to get some insurance runs, and with the heart of the order due up, it certainly was in the cards. Al Walston looked at the scorebook, saw who was due up for the Mets, and opted to bring in Ken Whelan to pitch. Whelan's first batter was Jamal. Perhaps Whelan was overthrowing, but none of his pitches were near the plate, Jamal walking on four straight. Manager Walston was pacing in the dugout, hoping his move didn't backfire. Frankie stood in and took a strike. The next two pitches were off the plate, and Frankie, sensing that Whelan might ease up a bit on his velocity to get it over, timed the delivery perfectly and sent a liner over third. Billy Jones, now in left, was playing the Met sluggers deep, and although he got to the ball on a couple of hops, Jamal went all the way to third and Frankie slid into second for a double. Time was called, and Walston went out to the mound to try settling Whelan down and to discuss strategy with first base open. Pitch to Panzini, or walk him to set up a force at any base? It was decided that with Whelan struggling with his control, he would pitch to Vince, but very carefully, not giving him anything good to hit. He also had his infield playing in for a play at the plate.

While this was going on, Joey motioned Vince over for a little chat of their own.

"Vince, I have a feeling they will pitch you down and away, not giving you anything good to swing at, so don't chase anything."

"Okay, Coach."

"I know you have been jawing with Jefferson all game. Keep it to yourself now and just concentrate up there, okay?"

"I know, let sleeping dogs lie. My dad loves to say that to me."

Vince heeded Joey's advice, kept his mouth shut, and never saw a strike, walking on four "unintentional-intentional" balls. That loaded the bases for Elliot. The Met dugout was on their feet, whooping it up and banging on the protective fence in front of them. Elliot laced the first pitch, a screaming line drive that was speared by Whelan, who turned and fired it to Parks as he stepped on the first base bag. Vince, like Jamal and Frankie, had been off with the crack of the bat, and was in no man's land. Just like that, two outs, runners at second and third. Ron, no doubt overanxious, swung at a 2-2 pitch out of the strike zone, for out number 3. Incredibly enough, the Mets had squandered a golden opportunity to pad their lead. Elliot had made a strong bid for at least one, maybe two RBI's, however it went into the scorebook as nothing more than a line drive double play. Baseball games are often decided on how teams perform in clutch situations. There was not much Paul, Billy, and Joey could say to each other or to the team at this point. Only silent prayers for good fortune.

Ryan warmed up on the sidelines in case he was needed, and Jamal completed his warmup tosses for what would be his final inning of mound work today. Leadoff batter Ted Kalinsky was up first, and he grounded one in the hole between first and second. In what was becoming a late inning routine, Dennis ranged far to his left, speared it and wheeled to throw to Elliot in time to get the speedy Kalinsky.

"Way to go, Dennis," shouted Paul.

Gil Felson was up next, and he poked one to right field. Lamar was playing deep, defending against a gap shot and a would-be extra base hit, and it took all his skill and speed to sprint in and make the grab. Two outs now, and that brought up Dave Willis. Willis had accounted for the Dodgers' only run so far with that first inning homer.

Paul, Billy, and Joey had the same thought- this was Jamal's game to win all the way. Jamal turned away from the plate to compose himself, took a deep breath, and went to work on Willis. Vince gave Jamal a low target. Joey positioned the outfielders deep and shaded around towards left. Jacob was just a few steps from the third base foul line, Ron way over in left center, Lamar shifted very far from the first base line, in right center. Jamal for one of the few times today, uncorked a pitch that sailed over Vince's head and outstretched glove for ball one. Vince moved his glove to the outer edge of the plate, and Jamal put it right there, as Willis swung and made contact. Confounding the shift, it was a line drive over first base, and after landing fair, started tailing into foul territory. Willis was running at full tilt, and to compound the situation, Lamar's first step in the direction of the ball caused him to stumble. With the play in front of him as he approached second, Willis was running like a freight train. By the time Lamar got to the ball, Willis was already between second and third, and with two outs, there was no stopping him now. Lamar relayed it to Dennis, who turned and threw to Vince, but it was not in time, a sliding Willis crossing the plate with the tying run. Pandemonium broke loose on the Dodger bench.

"Joey," shouted Vinnie at the fence, "He missed second base."

"Yep, saw that, Vinnie. Just waiting for the ball to go back into play."

Jamal was beside himself, overcome with emotion for having let the team down, and Billy yelled out for Jamal to pay attention to Joey. Praying that the base umpire saw it, Joey instructed him to get back on the mound with the ball, ask the home plate umpire if the game was back in play, and step off the pitching rubber to throw to Dennis at second who would tag the base. As the course of action unfolded, Jamal did as he was told to, and when the base umpire raised his right fist and shouted "Out", the game and series was remarkably over, in the strangest of circumstances.

Al Walston charged out of the dugout and ran right at base umpire Len Chisholm. Walston shouted that a game of this magnitude should not be settled like this and could not understand how Chisholm was so sure of the call. "Ask the other ump," demanded Walston. Chisholm shot back- Willis had missed the bag by a mile, and it was his (Chisholm's) obligation to call the play as he saw it, regardless of the situation. At the end of the day, it was his call alone to make. Walston retreated slowly back to the dugout, visibly distraught. His assistant Sam Parks was sympathetic but gave it to him straight. "Al, it wasn't close. I clearly saw it from my vantage point, but it happened so fast, the crowd was so loud, I just hoped they would miss it. They didn't. It's a tough way to lose. This one will hurt. We need to talk to Dave now. He's not in a good state of mind."

It took a lot for the deflated Dodgers to line up and shake hands with the Mets, but they did. Paul, Billy, and Joey were extremely gracious. Billy asked Al's permission to speak to Dave, to give him some advice. Al agreed- knowing that Billy's words would hold more meaning than his ever could at this moment, based on his notoriety alone. Billy shared with Dave that from what he saw of him all season, he was destined for greatness, and to try to use this as a stepping stone to what promised to be the first of many chances for him in the game of baseball. He himself had suffered through many losses and tried to learn something from each of them. Willis, wiping his eyes, just nodded back, because like most 12-year-olds in this scenario, he didn't have the words to thank him.

During this bizarre game ending, the Mets were feeling happy but uneasy. Paul sensed it and addressed it in his postgame chat. "Guys, I know, it was a strange way for the game and series to end, but we earned this victory. Now, let's focus on the positives. Jamal, you pitched a hell of a game. As a team, we made zero errors today. We had that lost opportunity to break open the game in the sixth and didn't, but only because Elliot really tattooed the ball, right into Walston's glove. A runner being called out for missing the base is just part of the game. I'll have the schedule for the finals tonight or tomorrow and will email everyone. Hey, we're playing for the championship! Bask in the moment- you should be proud of yourselves. You played a great game."

Joey walked to the parking lot with Vinnie, who started reminiscing. "Two semi-final deciding games, 25 or so years apart, and both ending in Bizarro Land." Laughing as he continued, "This feels awfully familiar."

"Yeah, the players have changed, Vinnie, but when you wear the Met uniform, nothing comes easy. Hey, been meaning to tell you, Vince is a real good player, both defensively and offensively. I even saw some of his old man's trash talking antics out there today."

"To tell you the truth, Joey, with me getting thrown out of the league, and embarrassing him in the process, he may have been making a conscious effort to tone down the rhetoric. But, a game like today can bring out the worst, or let's say the best, in a Panzini."

"Good one, Vinnie. See you soon."

"You got it, buddy. Take care."

The two ex-teammates got into their cars, and as Joey put the car into gear, he could not suppress a grin.

Chapter 37

The next morning, Paul received the schedule for the best 2 out of 3 finals, and it broke out in a way that was beneficial to the Mets. Because of scheduling conflicts in the lower leagues, there would be no games the remainder of this week, meaning Jamal could pitch game 1. It would be next Wednesday at 5PM, followed by Saturday at 11AM for game 2, and if necessary, next Tuesday at 5PM for game 3. Placing a conference call to Joey and Billy, they decided on a Saturday morning practice this week. As for practice between games one and two, they all felt it might be an overkill with the relatively short turnaround time, so they would be nixing it. Lastly, they agreed that if there was a game 3, they would hold a practice that Monday. Pitching rotation would be as it had been for the semi's: Jamal, Ryan, Jamal.

"Hey, guys", Paul said, "I could not get to sleep last night. The game was such a roller coaster, and to have it end the way it did, well, I suppose in a way it was fitting. I know you're never supposed to settle for anything in sports but based on how far we've come as a team, I have to think we're playing with house money from this point on."

"That can be a blessing or a curse, Dodsy," Billy replied. "On the one hand, maybe the kids subconsciously are also thinking along those lines, and the pressure will be off them, having gotten to the championship round. That part's good; they'll be loose. But, by the same token, what we must guard against is complacency and a feeling that they are lucky just to be here. I would like to think that what got them this far is that pedal to the metal mentality. Let's do what we can to try to instill that in them. Sure, they have probably overachieved, but there is no reason why they can't go all the way."

Joey added: "We want them to be relaxed, sure, but we do not want them to be in awe of the Pirates. We should make it crystal clear in practice that we mean business. They belong in the finals, and that they need to continue to do what got them this far."

"You guys are right, and of course they will never hear from me that we are settling. But you do have to admit, when we assembled for the first practice, reaching the finals seemed a bit beyond our wildest dreams. Win or lose, it has been a great ride these last weeks. I'll get the emails out now; see you both on Saturday."

Chapter 38

In what seemed like years since they last played against each other, the Mets and Pirates arrived at the field an hour prior to the 5:00 start of Game 1. The teams had split their two games in the Fall season, the Mets winning the first one 5-3, the Pirates victorious in the rematch 9-1. Pirate manager Dan Murchinson spent a considerable amount of time at practice this week preaching to his team to be confident, but not too overconfident; this was, he told them, a good Met team that they would be facing, with two quality starting pitchers in Jamal Jeffries and Ryan Bernstein.

From the Mets' perspective, they knew the Pirates presented a far superior offensive juggernaut than the Dodgers did, and hitters 1 through 9 in their batting order were all strong. It was almost like they presented an all-star lineup, mused Paul. Although the Pirate starting pitchers Frank Carruthers and Hadley Thomas were not as good as what the Dodgers had thrown at them, they were certainly effective, and as Paul knew, the Mets only scored one run the last time they played each other. For the Mets to win, they'd have to have hot bats to keep up with the Pirate attack, matching them batter for batter. It wouldn't be easy, but Paul liked the scrappiness of his ballclub, and perhaps destiny was on their side. Billy reminded Jamal that he could go up to 6 innings today. But, as expected, Billy exhorted him to hold nothing back against these robust Pirate batters.

The Mets were designated as the visiting team today, and following their pregame fielding drill, the team assembled in the dugout for some last-minute instructions from their coaches. Joey led it off.

"Guys let the game come to you. Let's be aggressive at the plate, but if Carruthers' control is not there, let's not help him out by swinging at bad pitches. In the field, expect their hitters to be aggressive regardless of the count or the score. Keep the balls in front of you and keep your heads in the game. Right Billy?"

"Exactly. There should be no pressure today. The pressure was making it to the finals, which you did. There is a reason you are here. Never for a minute should anyone feel like we don't fully deserve to be here. The best teams are the ones here today. Let's give it your best effort out there."

Paul didn't have much to add. "The game will dictate how we position you in the field. Back each other up in the outfield. Let's have a great game."

Carruthers finished his warmups and the game was set to begin. Ben led off the game, and after looking at a called strike one, continued his terrific hitting of late with a clean single up the middle. Jamal was next and he sent a screaming line drive to center, but it was right at Gerald Linton. A hard out, but an out just the same. With Frankie up, Carruthers uncorked a wild pitch and Ben took second base. On a 2-1 count, Carruthers took a little something off, and it had Frankie way out in front, popping up to shortstop where Bobby Baylor caught it for out number two. With first base open, Carruthers pitched carefully to Vince, who walked. That brought up Elliot, who came through, singling to left, Ben scoring, Vince taking second. But the rally ended there as Ron bounced back to the mound.

In the bottom of the inning, the Pirates got it back and then some. After retiring Logan Brockhammer, Jamal plunked Baylor on the forearm with a pitch, then saw Steven Lynch take him deep to left center, a one hopper to the fence. Baylor scored all the way from first as Lynch pulled into second. Rich Ortega, swinging from the hips, saw his bid for an extra base hit caught in the right centerfield gap by Lamar, Lynch smartly tagging up and making it to third, where he scored the go-ahead run on a base hit by Alvin Bean. Jamal came back to fan Linton for the third out. 2-1 Pirates, both teams showing early signs they would mean business with the lumber all game long.

In the top of the second, Jacob grounded one that had "seeing eyes" as it hopped between short and third and into left for a base hit. Hank tried bunting for a base hit, but it was corralled by Carruthers, who threw to first for the out, Jacob going to second. Lamar had difficulty getting around Carruthers, but managed to fist it to the right side, and nearly beat it out, Bean fielding the grounder and getting to the bag before Lamar by a step. With Jacob on third now, Ben lined it into center for another hit and that knotted the score at 2 apiece. Jamal had crushed the ball the first time with nothing to show for it, but this time he was more fortunate. He grounded a ball to second that Brockhammer assumed would hop up to him, but instead it skidded under the glove for an error, Ben going all the way to third. Frankie took a pitch to allow

Jamal to steal second, Ortega not risking a throw. On a 1-1 pitch, Frankie hit it hard but right at shortstop Baylor for the third out.

With the score knotted, Calvin Plunkett opened the Pirates' half of the inning with a clean single to left. Carruthers helped his own cause with a semi-line drive to right for a base hit. Lamar got it back in quickly, keeping Plunkett at second. Ed Lawrence was struck out by Jamal, but Brockhammer smashed one to Hank at third who bobbled it, had no play at third, ultimately held onto it, and all hands were safe. With the bases now loaded and only one out, Joey positioned the infielders at the corners to play in a few steps but had Frankie and Ben play at normal depth. Billy decided to pay a trip to the mound to settle Jamal down. Jamal's pitch selection to Baylor was terrific, and he fanned him for out number two. The dangerous Steven Lynch was up now, and with the infielders now at their normal depth, and with the outfield playing it deep, Jamal got the best of him, Lynch lofting a lazy fly ball to Jacob. Glad hands all around as the Mets got back to the dugout; the team knew they had dodged a serious bullet.

Vince led off, and singled sharply to right center. Elliot followed with a ground ball to short that Baylor gobbled up and stepped on second for an unassisted force play, but his throw to first was just a hair late to get a hard-running Elliot. Ron timed a Carruthers change up perfectly and lined it to left where it dropped in front of Plunkett for a hit. With runners on first and second, Paul allowed Jacob to hit rather than making a substitution at this juncture, and Jacob rewarded his manager's faith in him by tapping a slow roller towards second that landed in no man's land for an infield hit, loading the bases.

Paul called for Ryan to pinch hit for Hank. Dan Murchinson yelled out to Carruthers to throw hard from the Pirate dugout and had his infield play halfway. Ryan lofted it to left, but it was not deep, and when Plunkett made the catch with his momentum carrying him forward, Joey held Elliot at third. Two men out now, and the Pirate infielders retreated to their normal positions. Paul thought about pinch hitting for Lamar here but preferred having his speed at the plate just in case needed. Lamar worked the count to 3-1 and Carruthers laid one into Lamar, taking all the way, to run the count full.

With chatter at a high decibel among the three runners, the fielders, the benches, and the spectators, Paul looked like he had scripted this himself when Lamar's ground ball to short was bobbled momentarily by Baylor, negating the chance for a force at second. Baylor hurriedly threw to first but could not get the speedy Lamar. All runners were safe, and the Mets had a 3-2 lead. Carruthers came back nicely against the sizzling Ben, getting him to pop up to third for out number three.

The Pirates did not get their reputation as heavy hitters for nothing, and they wasted no time against Jamal in the bottom half of the third. Ortega and Bean doubled in succession, tying the score. After Linton grounded to second for the first out with Bean taking third, Plunkett singled sharply to left to drive in the go-ahead run, and he in turn came around to score when Carruthers placed one perfectly on an inside out swing, the ball landing over the head of Warren Cameron, now in the game playing first base, just inside the chalk along the first base line.

By the time David Dodsworth, shaded towards right center, could come up with it, Carruthers was standing on third with a three bagger. The scoring continued as pinch hitter Hadley Thomas got one over Frankie's head for a single. With the top of the Pirate order up now, the Met coaches conferred about relieving Jamal, but ultimately decided to let him continue. The decision worked out, with Jamal getting Brockhammer on a called third strike. Baylor was next and his bid for an extra base hit was thwarted by a diving catch in center by Ron. Three outs, but now the Pirates were on top 6-3 and they were hitting Jamal hard.

After the teams traded runs in the 4th inning, the Mets came up in the fifth trailing by a score of 7-4. Robert LaChance, Ryan Bernstein, and David Dodsworth each were retired in order. The score was still close, but Billy did not like what he was seeing from Jamal, and he suggested that Paul bring in Elliot to relieve. Allowing them to already think ahead to game 2, with Ryan having earned the right to start, the feeling was to keep him under wraps for today. Of course, the fact that Jamal was not exactly "setting the world on fire" in this game made the Ryan option more plausible. So, it was Elliot who got the call. Elliot would be pitching to the tail end of the Pirate order, and other than a one out single surrendered to Carruthers, did a nice job of keeping the Pirates at bay. The question was, could the Mets stage a last inning rally?

Dennis O'Brien led off the sixth and tried to get on base via the bunt route. His attempt at pushing it past the mound and towards second did not work out as planned; Carruthers was able to get to the ball and fire a strike to first for the first out. That brought up Jamal, and he helped the cause with a sharp hit to left, and when the ball took a funny hop, he was able to make it to second for a double. With the tying run in the on-deck circle, Dan Murchinson paid a visit to the mound, just to calm Carruthers down and remind him to concentrate on the batters, as Jamal's run alone meant nothing. The Pirates had Hadley Thomas warming up on the sidelines, but this was Carruthers' game to finish, felt Murchinson.

He did just that, retiring two tough batters in Frankie and Vince, both on fly balls to center. After lining up to shake hands, the Mets returned to the dugout. Neither Paul, Billy, nor Joey knew quite what to make of this game. It was a relatively close final score, but once the Pirates had busted out for those four runs in the 3rd inning, it never felt like the Mets were going to seriously challenge. Plus, that marked two straight games against the Pirates where they had had their way with Jamal, as hard as he was throwing. Perhaps we'd have more success with a pitcher like Ryan, who the Pirates had not seen on the pitching rubber since the Spring season, and who threw with less velocity than most of the starters in this league. Maybe, just maybe, his off-speed pitches would get them out of sync.

Trying to set just the right tone, the Mets coaches alternated speaking, and applauded their good hitting and overall defense. Tempering the Pirates' hitting assault, Joey praised Jamal for battling, and keeping the team in the game. Cliches were employed: "We'll get them next game" ...." This series is far from over". Billy even tried lightening things up with: "We've got them right where we want them", testament to the fact that the Mets seemed to respond better when their backs were up against the wall. That one had the boys cracking up. After they were dismissed and the three coaches started walking towards their cars, one thing was so clear, it didn't need to be spoken aloud: These were not the Dodgers they were playing against. These Pirates were tough. It seemed difficult to imagine they could be shut down offensively; the Mets would have to match them with the bats.

Chapter 39

It was an unseasonably cool day on Saturday and the air had an Autumn feel to it, perhaps more conducive to throwing a football around rather than a baseball. But this was no time for the Pirates and the Mets to be thinking about touchdowns; they had serious unfinished business to take care of on the diamond. Both teams would be sending their second starters to the hill: Ryan Bernstein for the Mets, Hadley Thomas for the Pirates. On the Met side, the coaches knew what to expect from Ryan based on his history: Pinpoint control, not a lot of strikeouts. They were hopeful that this change of pace in speed vs. Jamal and Elliot would throw the Pirates off their game a little.

On the other side, Dan Murchinson was confident in Thomas, a left hander with decent speed and control. In the four regular season games, the Mets only saw Thomas once, when he relieved Frank Carruthers, and that was back in the Spring. In situations of unfamiliarity, the slight edge usually goes to the pitcher. In the Met dugout, Paul told his team to watch Thomas' warm up throws, to get a sense of his delivery and speed. Teams were not permitted to stand behind the backstop, thus precluding any Mets from watching Thomas throw from that vantage point. Paul did not want to take any aggressiveness from his players, so he told them it was up to them if they felt more comfortable taking the first pitch this time. The Pirates had faced Ryan twice in the first half. Murchinson reminded them they would not be seeing much in the way of speed, but that Bernstein would always be around the plate.

The Mets were the home team today. As was customary in a game 2 final round, the league officials had transported the trophies to the field in case the Pirates won today, but out of respect to the Mets, kept them under wraps for now. As the Mets took the field, Joey had a careful eye trained on the body language of the Met players and he liked what he saw. Outwardly at least, he could not spot any apprehension or tenseness. They seemed to carry a relaxed yet business-like air about them. How that would translate to the game itself, he'd find out.

Logan Brockhammer led things off for the Pirates, and wasted no time, swinging at Ryan's first offering, smashing it to third. Jamal, showing outstanding reflexes, backhanded the one hopper, and threw to first for the

LONG MAY YOU RUN

out. Bobby Baylor, on a 1-2 count, whiffed on a pitch that was probably low, but too close to take. Steven Lynch then tried taking Ryan deep, but it stayed up there long enough for Jacob to grab it in left for the third out.

Lefty Hadley Thomas completed his tosses in the bottom of the inning. He threw with a three-quarter release and disguised the delivery a little by keeping the ball in his glove for as long as possible. Ben, leading off, was super confident, based on the hot streak he had been enjoying in the playoffs, and he opted to take a strike to time Thomas' deliveries. On a 2-1 pitch, Ben stroked it right up the middle, past Thomas, and into centerfield for a lead off hit.

Jamal took a pitch for ball one and then brought the bench and the spectators to their feet with a tremendous blast to left that landed over the fence for a two-run homer. The Mets were far from done - Frankie stroked a single to left and Vince followed with a liner over third. Plunkett in left had been playing Vince deep, and his throw into second kept Vince at first while Frankie, running all the way, scampered to third. That brought Dan Murchinson out for a visit with his pitcher, reminding him that it was only the first inning, and to try and keep things at bay. With Elliot up, Joey simultaneously flashed him the take sign as well as the steal sign to Vince. Ortega did not risk a throw to second. On a 2-2 pitch Elliot, looking overanxious, swung at one out of the strike zone for the first out. But Ron grounded it in the hole on the right side, and while Brockhammer made a nice play to get to the ball, his only play was to first, Frankie scoring and Vince moving to third.

With Ryan now up, Thomas uncorked a wild pitch; Vince decided with two outs to try to score, but Ortega recovered nicely, dove back to the plate, and tagged Vince out. As he returned to the bench to put on his catching gear, Billy put his arm around him and told him he liked the aggressiveness, and that it was the right play with two outs. Vince seemed to appreciate the gesture, as a smiling Vinnie looked on from beyond the fence.

It was Ortega, Bean, and Linton up for the Pirates, all sluggers. Ryan, as advertised, was keeping his pitches down, and he succeeded in getting each of the batters out, Ortega and Bean both skying to Ron in center, Linton popping up in foul territory to Jamal. So far, so good for the Mets, who were getting all they could have asked for from Ryan.

Ryan led off the bottom of the second, and he drew a base on balls. Jacob, timing Thomas' delivery perfectly, lined a ball over Baylor's head at short, placing runners at first and second. It brought up Lamar in a sacrifice situation and indeed he laid it down, but it did not go far enough, and Ortega was able to pounce on it and fire to third base for the force. That brought up the top of the order.

Ben continued his streak and placed one beautifully into short right field. Frank Carruthers picked the ball up on the second bounce and threw a strike to the plate, Joey smartly holding Jacob at third. Bases loaded now, only one out, and Jamal up. Murchinson thought about relieving Thomas but his options were not great, plus bringing in a pitcher in the middle of an inning and with the bags full is not an ideal situation, so although he did go out to the mound, it was more of a pep talk to settle Thomas down. With play back in, Thomas figured Jamal would be swinging from the hips so to speak and tried his best to pitch him low and away. Maybe Jamal would chase one that was out of the zone.

Jamal was patient, and to the dismay of Murchinson, he walked, bringing in Jacob with the fourth run of the game. Frankie worked the count to 2-0, took a strike, then sent the next one on a line to center. It was caught by Linton, whose only throw was to third, Lamar having tagged up to score. Vince made a strong bid for an extra base hit, but his fly ball was caught by Plunkett for the third out.

Paul cautiously wanted to see how the Pirates were going to react, so he kept his starting team in there as the game moved to the third inning. Ryan made quick work of Plunkett, but Carruthers reached out and poked a single to left for the first Pirate hit and baserunner. Thomas helped his cause with a slow roller down third that he beat out, Jamal unable to get to it in time. Brockhammer, at the top of the order, pounded one in the ground, Frankie grabbing it and alertly flipping to Ben at second for the force. Runners at the corners and two outs now. Bobby Baylor, a strikeout victim his first time, was not going to be denied this time, his base hit to left plating Carruthers. That brought up Lynch and brought Billy out to the mound to talk to Ryan and Vince.

"Ryan, he is going to look for a pitch he can drive over the fence. Let's try to keep it inside on him so he cannot get his arms fully extended. Also, in case of a base hit, back up third, okay?"

Ryan nodded, hitched up his belt, and went to work on Lynch. Billy could not have scripted a better series of pitches if he had tried, and with Ryan throwing in radar-like fashion, he threw a 1-1 pitch to Lynch who did not get enough wood on it, resulting in a "mile high" fly ball, and an easy catch in left by Jacob for the third out. Ryan was greeted on the dugout steps by a beaming Billy.

Paul pinch hit for Elliot with Warren in the bottom of the third. Holding a four-run lead, though precarious based on who the opposition was, he wanted to get the subs in as early as possible. Thomas mowed Warren down on three straight strikes. Ron popped up to second, Ryan grounded out to third, and quickly, the inning was over.

The term "economic" has an application in baseball, denoting a pitcher who gets through an inning or a game with a very low pitch count. Ryan was proving to be an "economics major" so far. His strike to ball ratio was outstanding, and the free-swinging Pirates were factoring into the equation by often swinging at the first pitch they saw. Although Ortega singled to lead off the fourth, Bean, Linton, and sub Steve Murchinson were retired on just five total pitches.

In the bottom of the frame, Robert LaChance and David Dodsworth were easily retired by Thomas. Paul hated having to take Ben out but needed to get Dennis O'Brien into the game. Dennis made the most of his plate appearance, fouling off several pitches before working out a walk, and took second on a wild pitch with Jamal at the plate. Thomas knew to work carefully here and wound up walking Jamal too. Frankie then delivered a clutch two out single, Dennis beating the throw home with a nice hook slide. Vince did everything he could to break the game wide open, but he just didn't get enough of it, and his fly ball was caught in center by Linton for out number three. As Ryan took the ball for the start of the fifth, nursing a 6-1 lead, Pirate skipper Murchinson called his team over.

"Guys, Bernstein is not going to overpower you and he is going to be around the plate. I love your aggressiveness but let's mix things up a little and take a strike. Let's face it; no matter if he is ahead or behind in the count, he is not going to blow one by you. And, you guys on the bench, I want to hear some noise. Let's see if we can unnerve him. Got it?"

Ryan would be facing three substitute players. Herb Klinger led things off, and he grounded out, Frankie to Warren. Oliver Allison was next, and he tried bunting his way on. But it was bunted too far, and a charging Hank, now in at third, threw him out. Matt Phillips kept the inning alive with a single up the middle, fielded by Jamal, now in center. Bobby Baylor was next, and on a 1-1 pitch he shot one into the gap in left center that landed between Robert and Jamal. Jamal made a nice play to get to the ball before it could reach the fence, and a strong throwback to the infield kept Phillips at third, Baylor pulling into second with a stand-up double.

This put the Mets in a quandary. Should they pitch to the dangerous Steven Lynch with first base open, or walk him? With two outs and still nursing a 5 run lead, the decision was to pitch to Lynch, albeit carefully. Lynch remembered that they had previously worked him inside and decided to adjust his stance ever so slightly to avoid getting jammed this time. Vince gave Ryan a low target, and Ryan didn't miss, but neither did Lynch, practically golfing one deep to left. The ball smacked the fence on a fly, both runners scoring and Lynch pulling into second with a clutch double. With the also dangerous Rich Ortega up, Billy felt it was time to bring in some heat. After conferring with Paul and Joey, they decided to bring in Elliot. Billy, now standing on the mound, told Ryan how proud he was of him, that he did an outstanding job, but it looked like he was a bit gassed now. Ryan walked to the bench and heard a rousing applause from the stands and the dugout.

Billy's direction to Elliot was simple: "Throw heat and throw strikes." Elliot completed his warmups, looked to Vince for a target, and went to work on Ortega, and on 2-1 pitch, the ball was pounded into the ground and through the legs of Hank. The high grass slowed the ball up a little, and Frankie, backing up the play, got to it in time to prevent Lynch from trying to score. With runners at the corners, Alvin Bean stepped to the plate, representing the tying run. Dan Murchinson had witnessed the Mets pull off their trick "Cutoff Play" against the Dodgers, and he yelled over to first base coach Pete Carruthers to keep Ortega there, rather than risk taking the bat out of Bean's hand in this spot.

The situation worked in the Pirates' favor anyway, with Elliot unleashing a wild pitch. Lynch raced about halfway down the line, but when he saw Vince quickly pounce on the ball, he retreated to third while Ortega did advance to second. That removed any possible force play. Bean then whacked one into center, a base hit that one-hopped in front of Ron. Lynch scored, but even with two outs, the ball was hit too hard for Ortega to be sent in, so he took the turn at third and held there. Now it was 6-4, runners on second and third. The deep Pirate lineup had another tough out in Gerald Linton. Paul took a quick look at his score book and noticed that on deck batter Herb Klinger had not played the required two innings in the field, meaning he could not be subbed out yet. Asking Billy to go out to talk to Elliot, Paul took the opportunity to converse with Joey.

"I know you are never supposed to put the go-ahead run on, but there is a huge difference in talent level between Linton and Klinger. I say we walk Linton. What do you think, Joey?"

"If we were only up by one, I wouldn't do it, because that would put too much pressure on Elliot, and a walk would tie up the game. But with a two-run lead, I agree; let's roll the dice."

When Billy got back to the dugout, he was brought up to speed, and as he turned to them and smiled, he said: "Yeah, it goes against conventional wisdom, but this Met team does nothing the standard way. Let's do it."

Billy shouted out to an unsuspecting Elliot, telling him to inform the home plate umpire that they were intentionally walking Linton. A buzz was generated in the crowd, as if to say, "What the heck are they doing?", with Linton trotting to first.

With bases loaded, Elliot pitched to Klinger. Figuring he'd be taking, Elliot took something off it, and it went for a called strike one. The next pitch was a high hard one, and Klinger foul tipped it. Perhaps overthrowing a bit, Elliot's next delivery sailed over Klinger's head, Vince doing all he could to get his mitt on it. Elliot paced on the mound, took a deep breath, and froze Klinger with a low hard one that caught the far corner of the plate for strike three. Paul high-fived Joey and Billy, and the first to congratulate a returning Elliot was Ryan.

Elliot was due to lead off the inning, as the Mets were looking for some insurance runs. His quality at bat ended with a base on balls. Ron was next, and his bid for a base hit was taken away on a diving stop at first on the second bounce by Bean, Elliot on to second. Hank was next, looking to atone for his fielding error. Atone he did, singling to short right field. Elliot was held at third. With Jacob replacing Robert here, Joey flashed the take sign and Hank remembered from practice what to do. Should the Pirates copy the Mets and attempt their version of the Cutoff Play or throw through to second, Hank's move was to get in a rundown between first and second, affording Elliot the opportunity to score. In the more likely scenario that the throw would just go back to the mound, Hank would put it into high gear and race for second. As it turned out, it was merely the latter, and with both runners in scoring position with one out, Jacob got the sweet part of the bat on a 3-1 pitch, forcing Klinger to retreat a few steps, thus in no position to throw home. His throw instead went to third, keeping Hank from advancing, but Elliot tagged up and scored.

Jacob was always coming through at the right time, and he heard it from an appreciative Paul as he took his seat in the dugout. Lamar would be pinch hitting for David now, and he walked. With a three-run lead, Paul decided to keep Dennis and his glue glove in there although he surely could have pinch hit with Ben. Ben was more than adequate with the leather, but Dennis was performing at such an elite level in the field, the decision was made to go with Dennis. He gave it a good shot, but his grounder to short was gobbled up by Baylor who touched second base for the third out.

As the Mets took the field for the sixth inning, Elliot would be facing 8,9, and then the top of the order. Frank Carruthers was up, and Elliot got the better of him, as a two-strike pitch was foul tipped into Vince's glove for the first out. Ed Lawrence was back in the game, and when he popped up to Hank, the Mets were one out away from tying up the series. But any possible celebration was stymied when Logan Brockhammer singled in the hole between short and third. Bobby Baylor, up next, kept the inning and the game alive when he stroked a clean single to center, Brockhammer to second. Now, who else but Steven Lynch up, representing the tying run. Benches and spectators alike were all on their feet, awaiting this confrontation.

This time, it was Lynch who succeeded. He sent a well-placed drive into right center. Ron and Lamar nearly banged into each other, which would have really spelled disaster, but they averted contact, Ron getting to the ball on two hops, spinning around and firing it to the cutoff man Frankie. Lynch was standing at second with a two-run double, cutting the lead to 7-6. With Ortega up and Bean to follow, Paul knew he could not play the intentional walk card now.

Vince ran out to settle Elliot down and the action was set to resume. While Elliot knew he had first base open, he did not want to walk Ortega and have to pitch to Linton with the potential tying and go-ahead runs on. Elliot's fastballs tended to rise, so Vince gave him an exceptionally low target. Ortega took the first pitch for ball one, then let a borderline pitch go by for strike one to even the count. The next one was well off the plate for ball two. Elliot got the following one over, with good velocity towards the outer part of the plate, but Ortega was ready for it, and lined it to right center, where Lamar was positioned perfectly, hauling it in for the final out. A raucous Met team rejoiced, as Paul, Billy, and Joey each breathed deep sighs of relief.

"Way to go, Mets. We are so proud of you," Paul started off in the dugout following the lineup for handshakes. "Look, it's no secret that those guys over there can hit, but you know what? We can and we showed it today. Ryan, you deserve the win, you were terrific, and a great job by Elliot in relief. Joey?"

"You know, I was watching each of you from the time we got to the field and throughout the game. You looked like a confident group, like you belonged, which is what we wanted to see."

Billy echoed those remarks. "A special shout out to Mr. Dodsworth, who called for the IBB on Linton. In the unlikely event you haven't noticed, nothing gets past your manager; nothing."

Paul, blushing, opted to take care of a little business now. "We'll be holding one last practice on Monday night. After all, in case you weren't aware, we have a final game to play on Tuesday."

"Snack bar on me, fellas," yelled Joey, to the bunch of happy kids as they raced to get in line.

Paul was packing up his stuff as he said to his cohorts, "We have some things to discuss for the next game. Let's talk tomorrow night; 7:30?" Billy and Joey nodded in agreement, both knowing what the subject would be: Who would be pitching for the Mets as they played for the championship?

Chapter 40

"Hey Billy. Joey is on another call, so he'll join us shortly. How's it going?"

"All good, Dodsy. Looks like we found a house and it's not far from you. You live on Corleaga Street, right? We'll be on Naomi Street."

"Yeah, Naomi is very close to me, we'll be neighbors! When do you move in?"

"Pretty soon. Hopefully, in a few weeks. It's been great being with my parents, but you know how it is; we want our own place."

"Yep, totally understand. I think Joey just got on the call. Joey?"

"Yeah, sorry. How are you guys?"

"Good, Joey. Billy, you want to tell him your news?"

"I was just saying that we found a place, on Naomi Street."

"That's terrific, Billy. Pretty close to where Dodsy lives."

"I know. We were just saying that."

"Anyway, Dodsy, you wanted to talk to us. I'm assuming it's about who we want to pitch the last game. Want me to start?"

"Sure, go ahead, Billy," Paul said.

"Based on what we've seen in the first two games, the move, in my opinion, is to start with Ryan. He had the Pirates off stride for pretty much the entire time he was out there."

"How do you think Jamal will take it, Billy?" expressed Joey. "After all, he has been our number one the entire time."

"I've already had a chat with him. He was disappointed, but mainly because he felt he let the team down, not that he deserved to get the ball. I'm glad to see he's thinking "team first" all the way."

"Let's put it this way," Joey said. "The Pirate offense is pretty stellar. It's doubtful either Ryan or Jamal will go all the way, so I was thinking back to what we decided the last time we were in this situation. We all agreed it was best to rotate hard, soft, hard, to keep the opposition off balance as much as possible, so my choice is Jamal, Ryan, Elliot in that order. Dodsy- you're the deciding vote."

"I'm leaning towards Joey's point of view. Yes, Ryan has out-pitched Jamal in the finals, but my gut tells me the Pirates will be more ready for Ryan and his slower stuff this time. My only question is, how will this affect your relationship with Jamal, not only as his coach but his Dad? What I mean is, if we give him the start, won't he feel that although his other coaches wanted him to take the mound, his own Dad was against it?"

Billy answered, in a lighthearted tone of voice that signaled to the others he had a smile on his face: "Guess that makes me the loser in this equation. He pitches, knowing his Dad was against it but got out-voted. Actually, he'll just be happy that it was decided he should start."

Joey replied: "If he's anything like his Dad, he'll take it the right way. Maybe he'll feel his Dad was just trying to be impartial."

Paul chimed in. "Billy, knowing you, you hedged your bet when you spoke to Jamal, that it was far from being written in stone. Why not just tell him you thought about it more, and the three-man staff ultimately decided this was the way to go?"

Billy answered. "Okay, guys. I wouldn't read all that much into this; like I said, bottom line, he'll be happy to get this chance. Now we've got to explain to Ryan why he is taking a seat. Any ideas?"

"I'm glad we scheduled that last practice for tomorrow," said Paul. "It'll be a lot easier to tell him in person ASAP, and not have to wait until game time. I think that we just level with him and tell him our thought process; kids respect that. Anyway, see you at the field."

As they hung up, each wondered if they were making the right call. Setting the massaging of egos aside, there was a championship on the line. Joey said sardonically out loud to only himself: "Hey, maybe we'll just outhit those guys and our pitching plans won't really matter." Not that he was buying into it, though.

Chapter 41

Billy let all three of their guns switch off in throwing batting practice, and as always, fielding practice, run by Joey, featured simulated game situations. Following the spirited practice, both Paul and Billy spoke to Ryan separately. They both agreed that Ryan took it well and he was not going to cause any trouble when they were this close to a championship.

Paul informed the team that win or lose, there would be a Pizza party at Vincente's on Tuesday night. As the equipment was being placed in Paul's trunk, Joey mentioned that he had already spoken to Vinnie and Ronald about having dinner at Vincente's on Saturday night, with the wives, and both said they were hoping to hear the Dodsworths and Jeffries' were as well.

"Hmm, two nights in the same week at Vinnie's place; that swelled head of his may grow even further," Billy chimed in.

"Yeah, he already thinks he's the only show in town," added Paul. "Sure, count us in."

"Okay, good, we're all set," Joey said. "Billy, Dodsy, I just wanted both of you to know what this whole experience has meant to me. It's truly been a godsend. I was in a pretty bad place, and now I'm having fun for the first time in years."

"I second that emotion," said Billy.

"I third it," chortled Paul with delight. "See you guys manana," as the three of them left in their cars.

Chapter 42

An overflow crowd was on hand to watch the big game on Tuesday. For the final time this year, the foul lines and batter's boxes were laid down. The bleachers were packed, with others sprinkled along the other side of the fence adjacent to the first base line. The Springtown Journal was well represented with a reporter and cameraman. League Commissioner Frank Covelesky of course was there and would be presenting all the trophies after the game. The Dodgers were all on hand, as they would be presented with their second-place trophies for the first half of the season. The Mets knew that they would be getting two trophies - one for their second-place finish for the back half, the other depending on the outcome today. The Pirates would be filling their mantles with three pieces of hardware - first place in each half, plus one of the awards based on today's final score. It was a great tradition, replete with pomp and circumstance.

The late afternoon sun was shining, temperature was in the high 60's, and after the pregame warmups, Paul Dodsworth and Dan Murchinson met at home plate with the umpires to go over the ground rules. The two skippers shook hands, wished each other luck, and scampered back to their respective dugouts.

As the Pirates were set to take the field and the Mets were getting ready to take their initial at bats, there was a real air of anticipation in the crowd. Would it be the big bats of the Pirates emerging victorious, or would it be the upstart, scrappy Mets?

Ben swung two bats to loosen up then dropped one, adjusted his batting helmet, and stepped into the batter's box. Frank Carruthers went into his windup and delivered a called strike. The game was on. Ben let the next two go by, both balls, and on a 2-1 count, grounded one past the outstretched glove of Bobby Baylor at short for a leadoff single. Jamal was next and he grounded one down the third base line, where a great backhanded stop by Steven Lynch prevented an extra base hit. However, Lynch's throw to first was not in time, and Jamal was safe, Ben advancing to second.

The Met dugout was very animated as Frankie stepped in. After taking a strike, he made a strong bid for extra bases with a drive to deep center, where it found the glove of a backtracking Gerald Linton. Jamal was playing it halfway and had to retreat to first, but Ben had heard Joey yelling to tag up, which he did and slid safely into third. With runners at the corners, Vince took the first pitch for a ball, and when Jamal ran to second, catcher Rich Ortega simply tossed it back to Carruthers, resulting in runners on second and third and only one out. For one of the few times this season in that spot, Vince did not come through, popping it up to Lynch at third for the second out. That left it up to Elliot, who picked Vince and the team up with a well-placed single to right, Ben scoring easily and Jamal right behind him with the second run. Carruthers, reaching back for something extra, ended the threat by striking out Ron.

Jamal sprinted out to the mound, trying to protect the early two run lead. Billy felt he did not need to remind him to hold back nothing. Logan Brockhammer was set to lead off, and after fouling off several pitches, Jamal got him on a swinging strike three. Baylor was next and he sent one into no man's land, dropping safely into short left field. Baylor took a big turn, forcing Jacob in left to make a hurried throw, and it was a wide one, sailing past Ben and into right field. Lamar smartly ran the ball back to the infield, Baylor now standing on second. If this unnerved Jamal, it was hard to tell, as he threw strike one to Lynch, followed by a beauty over the outside part of the plate that was fouled off. With two strikes, Lynch was prepared for anything, and when Jamal's next delivery was on the inner half of the plate, Lynch was ready and he drove it on a line drive over Jacob's head, one-hopping to the fence. It was a double, Baylor scoring easily. Ortega was next, and with Jamal making a good pitch, got the tough Pirate catcher to ground it to Ben, who tossed to Elliot for out number two, Lynch taking third. But Lynch was left stranded when Alvin Bean skied to center, where Ron hauled it in. 2-1 Mets after one inning.

Carruthers settled down nicely, getting Jacob, Hank, and Lamar in order in the top of the second. As Linton stepped to the plate to face Jamal, Paul paced in the Met dugout and wondered if any momentum the Mets had early on could be shifting towards the Pirates.

Jamal was throwing hard, but he walked the leadoff batter Linton, bringing up Calvin Plunkett. Plunkett hit it hard on the ground towards Ben at second who, perhaps expecting it to bounce up, uncharacteristically allowed it to go right through the wickets. Before Lamar could retrieve it, Linton was on third, Plunkett on first. Joey signaled to Vince and Frankie that the Cutoff Play was on. Carruthers did take the first pitch for strike one, as Plunkett ran for second. But, while Vince's throw went as designed to Frankie, Linton held at third.

"Guess they scouted us pretty well," Joey remarked with chagrin to Paul and Billy.

Carruthers then helped his own cause with a bloop over third. Linton scored to tie the game, Plunkett to third, Carruthers stopping at first. With Ed Lawrence bringing up the rear for the Pirates, they again had him take a pitch. In what could be termed a "videotaped replay", Vince fired to a correctly positioned Frankie, but Plunkett did not bite and stayed at third while Carruthers moved into scoring position.

Lawrence did not get good wood on the next pitch but his "swinging bunt" landed safely along the third base line, the Mets' only play being to see if it rolled into foul territory, which it did not. Plunkett scored, Carruthers to third. The only ball the Pirates hit hard so far this inning was the grounder by Plunkett that went for an error, yet they now had the lead, two men on and still no outs. Brockhammer at the top of the order was next, and this time, Joey, in a concession to the alertness of the Pirates, shouted to Vince not to even bother to try the Cutoff Play as Lawrence took second. Brockhammer did what he could as Jamal gave him very little to hit and fisted it between first and second. When both Elliot and Ben went for the ball, an alert Jamal tried to cover first, but alas he could not get there in time, and Brockhammer had himself a single and RBI, the Pirates taking a 4-2 lead. Brockhammer took second on the first pitch to Baylor. Billy then decided to call time and pay his son a visit.

"Jamal, they are not hitting you hard, so just keep doing what you've been doing and let's see if we can get out of this mess."

"Okay Dad."

As Billy stepped back into the dugout, he said to Paul and Joey: "Let's hope these even things out for us. It's like the Pirates are walking out onto the field and magically placing the ball in a perfect location each time." Unfortunately for the Mets, the magic of the Pirates continued.

The outfielders were playing Baylor deep, and he dunked one that dropped in front of Jacob for a hit, as the alert Pirate runners both scored. Another bloop single, but another two runs on the board for the Pirates. Billy conferred with Paul and Joey, and although the Pirates were not exactly tattooing Jamal, they agreed that maybe their fortunes would change with a different pitcher. So, Billy came back out to the mound and told Jamal what they were thinking. Because it was only the second inning, they could not yet remove any player from the field and bring in Ryan, so it was Elliot who they brought in to relieve, Lamar moving to first, Jamal to right. So much for the coaches' pregame plan of Jamal/Ryan/Elliot in that order, but sometimes game circumstances dictate different implementation.

Elliot had his work cut out for him, facing Lynch, Ortega, and Bean with one on and no one out and five runs already in this inning. Elliot had trouble with Lynch, ultimately walking him. There was a momentary reprieve when Ortega lined it to Frankie. One out, finally. But Bean came through for the Pirates, lacing a shot over third. Baylor came around to score, and Lynch tried to follow suit, but a great throw by Jacob nailed him at the plate. Bean took second on the throw home. Elliot retired Linton on a fly to right that Jamal caught. 7-2 Pirates after two innings.

With the top of the Mets order due up, they were hoping to eat into the Pirate lead, and although Ben, Jamal, and Frankie all hit the ball with authority, they had nothing to show for it, and in quick fashion, the Mets were back out on the field. Paul made some substitutions, the key one having Ryan take the mound in hopes he would stymie the Pirate batters, not that his predecessors had pitched all that badly. On the contrary, they were mostly victims of well placed, rather soft hits coupled with a few errors behind them. Jamal was back at third, Warren in at first, Dennis now at second, Robert in left, David in right.

Murchinson too made wholesale substitutions. Herb Klinger would lead off. With the Mets having been retired on only a handful of pitches in their half of the third, Ryan had little time to warm up and it showed, as his normal excellent control escaped him, Klinger walking on 5 pitches. Carruthers was next and he found a pitch to his liking, sending a "tweener" that skipped past Ron and rolled to the warning track. A strong throw kept Carruthers at second, but Klinger came all the way around to score. Hadley Thomas pinch hit for Lawrence and grounded out to Dennis, Carruthers advancing to third. Rick Smithers was in for Brockhammer, and Paul, Billy, and Joey could only shake their heads as Smithers dribbled one down the first base line and beat it out, Carruthers scoring. It didn't end there. Ryan ran the count full to Baylor, and on the next pitch, Baylor sent a slow roller to Frankie, who not only had no play at second, but threw late to first. Another well placed hit for the Pirates. Lynch was up now, and the Pirates were smelling blood. Billy paid a visit to the mound to settle Ryan down, reminding him that other than the Carruthers semi-line drive, everything else was of the light, well placed variety. Ryan went to work and Lynch, perhaps overanxious, swung at a pitch that was way over his head, chopping it to short, where Frankie charged in and made a strong throw to Warren for the out at first. Two outs now, with runners at second and third. Ryan may have dodged a bullet from Lynch, but Ortega's arsenal was fully loaded, and under the advice of Murchinson to be patient, waited for a pitch to his liking and grounded it cleanly into left, plating both runners. Matthew Philips, another sub, took a called third strike that was questionable to Murchinson, but with a big lead, was not about to get into it with the umpire and didn't utter a peep.

The inning was finally over, the Pirates now with a commanding 11-2 lead. Not only did the Mets find themselves way behind, they were in danger of having the game called if the Pirates were to add to their lead next inning. The Springtown Little League had a Mercy Rule, meaning that if a team were ahead by 10 or more runs after 4 or more innings, the game would be over, and this included playoff contests.

Joey pulled the team together. "Guys, we may be down by nine runs, but this game is far from over. Practically all the Pirate balls have not been hit hard. Now, I don't want any of you to go up there swinging for the fences and try to get back those nine runs in one shot. It doesn't work that way. Think of it like this, if we can get three runs an inning, and keep them at bay when they are up, we'll have caught up. Let's each take a strike and maybe we can work out some walks. I will leave it up to you if you want to lay one down for a base hit, but obviously not with two strikes on you. Lastly, I want to hear some noise on this bench. This game is not, I repeat, not over. Are you with me?" A rousing "Let's Go Mets" followed, and the bench did their best to get Carruthers off his game.

Vince stepped in, and faking a bunt, got things started with a base on balls. Warren was next, and he too walked. The families and friends of the Mets in the crowd started getting into it. Murchinson sensed complacency and overconfidence with his team in general and Carruthers specifically, and yelled from the top of the dugout steps to bear down and concentrate. The

Pirates were not expecting Ron to bunt, but he did, and beautifully, down the third base line. Lynch had no play and just held onto it, loading the bases with no outs. Robert LaChance did his name proud, looping one over first for a base hit. With the big deficit, Joey opted to play station to station ball, holding Warren at third as Vince scored. A very excited Robert high fived Billy, as Ryan stepped in. Trying to help his cause, he sent one deep to left. Klinger caught it, Warren tagged up and scored. Ron alertly tagged up too, and when the throw to third was way offline, he picked himself up and raced home to score another run. Robert had initially played it halfway, but after retreating to first, took second on the wild throw.

The Met bench was in a frenzy. Three runs were already in, and only one out. David was up and after taking a strike, he did all he could to move the chain line, but an excellent play behind the second base bag by Baylor on David's grounder resulted in the out at first, Robert to third. Dennis was now the batter, and Carruthers committed the Cardinal sin of uncorking a pitch in the dirt that hit Ortega's shin guard on a bounce, and caromed far enough away for Robert to race home with the fourth run of the inning. Carruthers, mad as all hell, stomped on the mound, then went into his motion and proceeded to mow Dennis down on strikes, ending the inning. But the Mets were inching closer, having sliced the lead from nine runs to five, heading into the bottom of the fourth.

Billy tried injecting a little levity in the dugout, as he noticed that Paul was wound tighter than a drum. "All that talk about how we were going to set up our pitching for today. We could have had Sandy Koufax on the hill for us and it wouldn't have mattered a lick; those balls they've been hitting have eyes, I tell you."

Joey, not missing a beat, replied: "Koufax, or Mr. Billy Jeffries of Detroit."

That loosened Paul up a little, who uttered such a loud guffaw, his scorebook went flying out of his hand. "That's what I love about you guys; always competitive, sure, but you have your heads on straight."

"What did Lou Skinner always preach, Dodsy? Play the game right, but always have fun."
"That he did, Billy; that he did."

As they moved to the bottom of the fourth, Steve Murchinson, in for Linton, led off, and he popped out to first. Klinger was up for his second time, and Ryan made quick work of him, inducing a grounder to Jamal. Carruthers, a dangerous batter, made Ryan pay for a pitch right down the middle, and it went high and deep, over the left field fence for a home run. After getting Lawrence on a comebacker to the mound for the third out, Ryan displayed atypical (for him) emotion as he got to the dugout and hurled his glove against the fence behind the bench. Billy was going to tell him that it was only one run, but thought the better of it, and let it slide. Maybe that's what the team needs right now, to get mad/get even, he felt.

Top of the fifth now, and Jamal was set to lead things off, Carruthers and the Pirates nursing a six-run advantage. Jamal got the Mets off to a good start with a clean single up the middle. Frankie was next, and he grounded one into the hole between first and second, where Bean, back in the game, made a fine stop and raced to the bag in time for the out, Jamal taking second. Vince then got his bench on their feet with a deep drive to left that hit the warning track, then bounced over the fence for a ground rule double, plating Jamal.

This brought Murchinson out of the dugout and to the mound. Most of the Pirate starters were now back in the game, but Murchinson, a thinking man's manager, had held back Hadley Thomas from reentering, and he was warming up on the sidelines. Murchinson signaled for Thomas, congratulated Carruthers for a job well done, and sent him to the outfield, where he replaced Lawrence. Thomas' first batter was Elliot, who was back in for Warren. Elliot greeted him by stroking one to deep right. Carruthers showed off his all-around skills by racing it down. Nice bid by Elliot, but just a long out, Vince retreating to second. Two outs now and Thomas was looking to end the inning, but Ron extended it with a grounder that glanced off Baylor's glove and into left field. By the time Plunkett retrieved it, Vince, racing all the way with two outs, scored ahead of the throw, Ron alertly taking second.

That was as far as Ron got. Jacob grounded it hard but right back to the box, where Thomas tossed it to Ben for the third out. The Mets had further cut into the lead, trailing 12-8, and now needed to keep the Pirates from doing further damage as the game moved to the bottom of the fifth.

It would be the top of the Pirate order: Brockhammer, Baylor, Lynch. Ryan induced Brockhammer to pop up to Ben at second for the first out. Baylor's bid for a base hit was negated on a spectacular back hand stab and throw by Frankie. With the outfield deep and shading Lynch to pull, and with the count at 1-2, Ryan's pitch was in a perfect spot on the lower outside corner, but the great Lynch did not miss it, sending a laser to right field. Lamar, the fastest player on the team if not the league, went into high gear and motoring towards the foul line, made a marvelous shoestring catch on the run. As he straightened his body up and the momentum carried him into foul territory, he braced himself against the fence. Two hard hits, well placed balls, two tremendous fielding plays. As the Met team assembled in the dugout, they embraced Frankie first, then Lamar. Ronald made a beeline from the bleachers to come close to the dugout and congratulate his son.

"Ronald", beamed Cousin Billy, "the only other person in league history who could have gotten to that ball is you."

"Ha, maybe 25 years ago, but not on these legs," Ronald replied.

Joey liked to take things in stride, but he did not want Frankie's great play to get unnoticed.

"Frankie, as one shortstop to another, that was a heck of a play, and I not only loved how you got to that ball, but how you steadied yourself and made such an accurate throw. So proud of you."

Paul, having to shout over an animated dugout, gave the batting order for the final at bat. "Ryan, Lamar, Ben, to start us off. We need baserunners, so let's take a strike, don't swing at bad pitches, and of course be ready to protect the plate with two strikes on you."

Ryan showed bunt to get Thomas off his game, and it worked, as he walked on 5 pitches. Lamar was next and after taking a strike, did what he does best, pounding one into the ground towards third and beating the throw. Just like that, the first two were on and should they get an additional base runner, the tying run would be at the plate. A game the Pirates led by 9 runs at one point was in fact turning into a nail biter.

Ben was next, and he smashed one, but right at Thomas, who in practically self-defense gloved the line drive. The ball was hit so hard, both runners had no time to even think about advancing, so no chance for Thomas to get more than a single out. But, a big first out, nevertheless.

Jamal stepped in as Joey shouted both encouragement and a reminder not to overswing. Jamal tapped his helmet in acknowledgement and steadied himself in the batter's box. Working the count in his favor at 2-1, he found a pitch in his wheelhouse and boy, did he get all of it. It was a deep line drive to left. Plunkett raced back, but he had no luck as the ball landed well over the fence. The entire Met team met Jamal at home plate as the crowd erupted. Incredibly, the Mets had clawed their way out of a deep abyss, and the deficit was now down to just one run.

That brought up Frankie but before the at bat could take place, Murchinson paid a visit to the mound to try to settle his reliever down. Reminding Hadley Thomas that they still had the lead, he told him to focus on the next few batters. Thomas was understandably shaken; who wouldn't be?

Murchinson returned to the dugout. Both he and Paul could be observed pacing back and forth. Those on the benches and those in the crowd tried to adopt any special positions for good luck. Others closed their eyes and did some silent praying. In the field, the Pirates offered words of encouragement to their pitcher, a few understandably hoping the ball would not be hit to them, or that if it was, that they would not commit a costly error. These were 12 and 13-year-olds. They could not be faulted for being nervous, with the momentum having shifted towards the Mets.

Joey took the timeout opportunity to call Frankie over, and told him that the automatic take sign until a first strike was off, but not to help Thomas out by swinging at anything off the plate.

As Frankie stood in, Thomas peered into Ortega, and his first delivery was outside for ball one. Thomas let up a bit on the next pitch, not wanting to go to 2-0, and Frankie was waiting on it, sending a gapper into left center. Linton did get to it on a fly, barely, but the ball did not stay in the webbing, falling safely to the ground. Frankie was busting it out of the box, and slid safely into second with a double, representing the tying run.

The dangerous Vince Panzini was next, and his normally verbose dad, caught up in the moment as well, could not bear to look. Vince looked over to Joey, saw that the take sign was removed for him as well, and planted his feet in the batter's box. With the count in his favor at 2-1, he smacked a hard grounder up the middle. Baylor made a real nice play to not only get to the ball but steadied himself and fired to Bean at first to nip Vince for out number two. Frankie watched the play as it unfolded, and not wanting to get tagged out by Baylor, waited until he saw the throw being made before taking off for third, easily making it as Bean decided not to chance a wild throw.

"Great try, son," yelled Vinnie. "You did all you could; the guy just made a great play on you."

It was now left up to Elliot Markow. The tying run was 60 feet away. Elliot gave himself a pep talk to be aggressive, but also not to swing at bad pitches. Murchinson shouted to Ortega to make sure to block anything low. The first pitch was a little low for Elliot's liking, and he did not offer on it, even though it got the lower part of the plate for strike one. The next two pitches were also low, and out of the strike zone. Elliot fouled off the next pitch, and the one after, then watched one that was high. The count was full. Elliot called time, settled himself, and dug back in. Not wanting to let a third strike go by, he fouled the next two pitches off; both would have been ball four. The next one was right down the middle, and Elliot could only get a small piece of it, foul tipping it. Had Ortega held on, it would have been strike three, but it went in and out of the mitt; just another foul ball as Paul breathed a sigh of relief. The next pitch was high, and Elliot exercised proper bat control, drawing the base on balls after a long, productive at bat.

As Ron strolled to the plate, Joey had a decision to make. He wanted to give Elliot the steal sign to not only get him into scoring position, but to eliminate any force out at second. But, what if this time, the Pirates did throw through and Elliot became the final out? Billy, sensing the situation, whispered to Elliot to keep one eye on Ortega, and if he did throw to second, to get in a rundown, allowing Frankie the opportunity to score first.

Ron looked down to Joey, saw he had the take sign, and Thomas made his pitch. It was a strike, and Elliot took off for second. Ortega, under instructions from Murchinson, had no intention of attempting to throw him out, and instead faked a throw to see if he could catch Frankie off third. Alertly, Joey shouted to Frankie to stay there. Thus, all hands were safe and the tying run at third, the go-ahead run at second.

"Focus on the batter, Hadley," exhorted Murchinson. "You get him out, we win."

Thomas nodded. But, sometimes, too much concentration can have the opposite effect, and his next delivery sailed inside, plunking Ron on the shoulder. It hurt, but Ron, wincing, sucked it up and trotted to first.

This brought up Jacob, hoping to put his team in the lead, or at the very least, tie the game up. Murchinson screamed out to his infielders that now there was a force at any base. Joey shouted out to the three runners to run hard on anything hit. Amidst the hysteria in the bleachers, Joey sensed a calmness in Jacob's demeanor, as he stepped into the box, dug in and awaited Thomas' serves. Thomas knew he could not walk the batter, and Jacob knew it too. Who would have the advantage of getting ahead in the count?

Thomas could not assume Jacob would be taking a strike, and thus did not want to just lay it in there, so with some real heat delivered a pitch that Jacob swung at, fouling it off to the right side. The next pitch was a tad outside, and Jacob was able to control himself and take it for a ball. Thomas missed with his next offering, and the count was 2-1. When the next pitch was out of the strike zone as well, Jacob had the count well in his favor, but the next pitch was not quite where he wanted it to be, so he took it for a called second strike.

The count was full. Joey reminded Frankie and Elliot not to leave too soon. Billy did the same with Ron. Thomas looked to Ortega, wound up and threw one over the plate.

Jacob connected and sent a vicious line drive over the third base bag that had base hit written all over it. But it was speared on the fly by a lunging Lynch, snatching the ball and the hopes of the Met contingent in one instant.

Whatever jubilation was felt by the Pirates was met with utter shock by the Mets. The Mets had fought valiantly against the Pirates, only to go down in defeat by the slightest of margins. Jacob and the team had done all they could to try to win this game, but how it went down would no doubt sting for a very long time. For what seemed like an eternity, the Mets all stood in a sort of suspended animation.

The teams lined up for the customary handshakes, with the Mets going down the line in a stupor, like they were in a trance. When Dan Murchinson got to Paul, Billy, and Joey, he was gracious. "You know, men, your team gave us everything we could handle and then some. You should be very proud of them."

Paul, hiding his disappointment with all he could muster, was equally amiable, and surprising himself, was able to put some words together.

"Dan, you have a hell of a team there. You may not know this, but the three of us were involved in our own struggle with the Pirates a long time ago. It was some rivalry back then, but your team here, nothing but respect for your players and you as a manager. Congratulations for a job well done."

Billy and Joey echoed those comments, and the three coaches walked back to the dugout to talk to their shaken squad, Joey placing his arm on Paul's shoulder.

Paul led things off, addressing all 14 boys who either had their heads down, had tears streaming down their faces, or a combination of both.

"Guys, I don't care what the final score reads. You are all winners in my book. Each one of you should be so proud of how you played, not just today, but all throughout the season and the playoffs. Think of it this way: That is a great team over there in that dugout; they waltzed to division titles in both halves. Not only did we take them to a third game, but we went from being down nine runs to coming so darn close to winning. Sure, I know, it hurts. Hey, it hurts me too. But you know what? We didn't lose by making a game deciding error. We didn't lose by striking out. We lost when a ferocious line drive was caught. I want each of you to leave here with your heads held high. You made all of us and your families proud. You played like champions."

"Boys," Billy added, "You know, I have had my share of moments, both on this field and in the biggest stadiums in the country. I have never felt such pride as I do now. As you all know by now, I have moved back to Springtown with my family. Of all the reasons I could think of for wanting to make this move, I could not have anticipated the degree of joy each of you gave me. From the practices, to the games themselves, I can honestly say you each gave it your all, and I am so grateful to have been associated with each of you. Joey- I'm sure you have some thoughts to share."

Joey took a moment, choosing his words thoughtfully. "I heard somewhere that there is no such thing as losing. There's only winning, and learning. I want you all to think about what you learned this season. I know for many of you, you learned that with a lot of hard work, and with some sacrificing for the good of the team, there is no limit to how far you can go. I know today's outcome was not the one we hoped for, and that will stay with you for a while, but believe me, it will subside, and then, what will be left? The memory of a wonderful experience and a lot of lessons you'll take with you always."

Ben, one of the 12-year-olds on the team, spoke up. "Mr. Jeffries, will you come back next year to coach us again?"

"Absolutely, as long as my two comrades are here by my side."

Chapter 43

The trophy ceremony was about to begin, Paul had the boys come together for one last rousing chant of "Let's go Mets". The families of the team, who made their way from the bleachers and approached the dugout, vociferously applauded with utter pride.

Commissioner Frank Covelesky stood at home plate, microphone in hand, and bridge tables behind him loaded with trophies. "Well, I must say, that was quite a thrilling conclusion to another great year for our Springtown Little League. I wish to thank the three teams here today - Pirates, Mets, and Dodgers for showing us excellence on the field and sportsmanship on and off it. I would now like to introduce the Dodgers and their manager Al Walston. The Dodgers finished in second place in the first half of the year and came so close to getting to the championship round."

After the Dodgers were given their trophies, Covelesky took back the microphone.

"Now, let me introduce the Met manager, Paul Dodsworth. Paul, I have to say, your team gave all of us so many thrills, and I would like to add, I don't believe I've ever seen a team so fundamentally sound. Paul, please take the mike and introduce your players."

"Thank you, Frank. Allow me to begin by congratulating both the Pirates and the Dodgers. It was a pleasure to be able to compete with two fine squads. We all tried to beat each other, but when the games were over, what remained was a mutual respect. I would also like to thank, from the bottom of my heart, my two coaches, Billy Jeffries, and Joey Harrison. Sure, I was the one who was filling out the lineup each game, but it was the two of them, my childhood friends, and wonderful players, who gave the team such incredible instruction and leadership. Of course, the kids were initially gaga to find out that an illustrious player such as Billy would be helping, but after a while, they saw that he wanted to be treated just like any adult. As for Joey, what can I say? The way he took to the task, the way he helped guide the team and his devotion, it reminded me of what our manager Lou Skinner, may he rest in peace, once said about Joey when he was introduced during the award ceremony so many years ago. I may be paraphrasing a bit, but it went something like this: 'Every coach should get to have a kid like him on their team at least once in their lifetime. He's just a joy to watch play because he loves the game so much.' I can attest to the fact that has not changed." Pausing, he beamed with pride in the direction of Billy and Joey, both of whom nodded back in appreciation. "Now, I'd like to introduce the Met players."

"This kid may not be the most talented player on the team, but he loved putting on the uniform every time, and he prided himself with keen knowledge of the sport, David Dodsworth."

"He got a big hit today, and showed a lot of improvement, Robert LaChance."

"Next is a player capable of playing multiple positions, and playing them well, Warren Cameron."

"This is a kid who we crowned Glue Glove. His fantastic plays in the field became the norm for him: Dennis O'Brien."

"A player who really improved as the season went on, and made some big plays for us, Hank Neilson."

"Keeping his family tradition alive, our speedster, and what a catch he made today, Lamar Carson."

"Our center fielder, the guy who is our captain in the outfield, Ron Dent."

"Without a doubt, the most improved hitter on our team, lately impossible to get out, Ben Caloway."

"He came oh so close to tying things up today, and he had his share of big plays too, Jacob White."

"A great hitter who also did an outstanding job for us as a reliever, Elliot Markow."

"One of our two top notch starting pitchers, and an excellent hitter in his own right, Ryan Bernstein."

"A tremendous all-around player who is a fine catcher and slugger supreme, Vince Panzini."

"You know, many years ago, the Mets had an amazing shortstop (pointing towards Joey) and I think he'd be the first to say that our current version is as good as it gets, Francisco "Frankie" Martinez."

"Lastly, he came to us at the start of the second half and helped turn our team around, not only with his outstanding skill set, but how he fit in with everybody from day one. A great pitcher and hitter, Jamal Jeffries."

Taking the mike again, Frank Covelesky said: "Folks, let's hear it for the Mets."

After the Pirates received their trophies, Paul reminded the boys that there would be a pizza party at Vincente's at 6PM tonight. The three coaches proceeded to walk towards their cars.

Billy said, "Dodsy, you were great at the mike. I just want to say, you did a wonderful job with these kids. You should feel really proud of yourself."

"Thanks, Billy. It's really quite simple when the ones helping you are the ones you look up to the most."

Joey added, "The way you know just when and how to substitute, how you watch the opposition and take all of that in; you know, I have to say, I've learned so much from you. I mean that."

"Well, thanks, guys. We really do make a good team."

"I am going to miss the 13-year-olds who will be moving on next year," added Billy. "Kids like Frankie."

"Ahem," Joey chimed in with. "I know a certain 11-year-old shortstop who will be wearing the Met uniform next year."

"Yeah, that's right. Will Harrison," said Paul. "That'll be something. The Jeffries and Harrison names, together again in the same lineup."

As they got into their cars, the ache they each felt earlier having subsided, it was replaced by a feeling of great accomplishment, pride, and mutual admiration for each other.

Chapter 44

The kids were in good spirits as they chowed down on pizza, baked ziti, and baskets of garlic bread. Spearheaded by David, they gave out their own "mock" awards, such as Worst batting stance and Slowest base runner. There was a lot of laughter and the chance to roast their teammates was a real lift for everyone.

The next morning, Paul woke up and reflected on the previous day. He was able to put the loss in the rear-view mirror and was now able to appreciate the season in its entirety. It was a magical run. He looked forward to the weekend dinner with the guys and their wives.

On Saturday, as each of them strolled into Vincente's, they were warmly greeted by Vinnie and Camille. They each made their way to the table, set up in a perfect spot, in the rear corner. The best in the house. After drinks arrived at the table, Joey stood and cleared his throat.

"Gang, I know we're here to celebrate an awesome season, but I also have some news to share. I want you all to know you are likely looking at the new Baseball Head Coach of the Springtown High School."

"That's fantastic, Joey," beamed Billy. "How did that happen?"

"Ralph Fesco. He was our high school coach," he explained to the wives. "His son Jack is now the school principal. He apparently remembered me from those days and came down to one of our playoff games. We got into a conversation about the high school team, one thing led to another and the next thing I knew, he was inviting me to interview for the Head Coach position, which was about to be vacant."

"Wow, that is unreal! But I thought you needed to be an accredited teacher to coach high school. Is that not the case?" Paul asked.

"Lucky for me, I majored in Education at UCLA and got my teaching certification, but never used it as I took over my Dad's sales rep organization. I just need to take a few online classes to get recertified and pass the New

York State exam. If all goes as planned, I'll be hired as a full time Phys Ed teacher, just in time for the next season. You know I was never cut out to be a salesman. This will keep me close to home, on full salary with benefits, plus extra compensation for the coaching gig. I want you all to know how much your support has meant to me. I was really lost for a long time and lost sight of what's important to me. I was just going through the motions. The experience of coaching the kids, reuniting with old dear friends, and now with this job on the horizon, I've done a 180-degree turn. I'll be doing what I love and getting paid to do it."

"That's so great, man," said Vinnie.

"Yeah, couldn't be happier for you, Joey," added Ronald.

Kim was teary-eyed, "You remember the movie City Slickers, where at the end the Billy Crystal character comes back home from his trip and tells his wife 'Look what I found', pointing to the smile on his face? That's what this journey has done for Joey," she shared. Her husband leaned over and gave her shoulder a squeeze.

Joey turned to Billy, seated next to him. "You know, there's going to be room for an assistant coach, and since you are, ahem, currently retired and unemployed...what do you say, Billy?"

"Joey, I appreciate the offer, but this is your turn to be in the spotlight. I'll be cheering you on from the stands".

"I had a feeling that would be your answer. I'll accept it under one condition. You agree to play on my softball team next year, just like old times. Me at shortstop, you in centerfield."

"Well, as long as we're quoting movies tonight, 'you made me an offer I can't refuse'."

Vinnie interjected: "Hey, what are we (his arm around Ronald), small potatoes? Can we get in on the action?"

"The more the merrier!" exclaimed Joey. "As long as you promise, Vinnie, to give us your best trash talk. Don't hold anything back."

Vinnie leapt out of his seat, came over to Joey, feigned a punch, and instead gave him a warm embrace.

A smiling Joey added: "Hey Ronald, the league allows a courtesy runner for a player nursing an injury. Guess we know who we'll be inserting in that spot."

Billy chimed in "Paul, you ready to be our scorekeeper again"?

Paul raised his glass. "I can't wait to pencil in each of your names again. Hey, how about this: We can be called the Skinner Squad." Everyone raised their own glasses and shouted in unison to the rafters: "Long Live the Skinner Squad!"

THE END

ACKNOWLEDGEMENTS

My inspiration for the book title came from watching the documentary: Do You Believe in Miracles? The Story Of The 1980 U.S. Hockey Team. As the end credits roll, the Neil Young song "Long May You Run" is heard. To me, the fit was perfect for both that doc and this book, as it not only spoke to me of holding on to those memories, but how the years cannot deny us the friendships we developed, and the importance of teamwork.

As in my earlier book A Season to Remember, liberties were taken with respect to how the baseball season was scheduled. In a (my) perfect world, there would be both a Spring and a Fall season, to add some extra drama.

I owe a tremendous debt of gratitude to several family members.

To my son Scott - After trying to find just the right storyline for this book, it was he who gave me the angle I was looking for. He also wrote what I think are brilliant lyrics for the Foreword, quite poignant and allegorical. It's a flat-footed tie for who is his biggest fan: His wife/my daughter-in-law Michelle, or me.

To my daughter Traci - An accomplished, amazing writer in her own right, she wholeheartedly agreed to proofread the book, and did a first-class job. When I first shared with her my idea for the book title, she was "all in".

To my son in law Sam - I needed his advice on some music references from his generation and he was there to guide me. One thing about our family - We could be trivia lifelines for pop culture, and Sam is as good as it gets on music and movies from the 80's on up.

To my brother Tommy - From the time he wiggled his legs to distract the pitchers in his infancy PAL days, his zany outlook on life took him on a career trajectory that always seemed to be a natural progression. TK gave me greatly appreciated support in getting the book started.

Lastly, to my wife Joy - She probably knows me better than I know myself, and she pushed me to do a second book, realizing that I would have a blast writing it, and as usual, she was right. An amazing artist, it was her vision for the concept of the book cover design.

ABOUT THE AUTHOR

LES KOENIG has spent close to 50 years in the Housewares industry and while he has traveled extensively the world over, baseball is his first love. A graduate of Queens College in New York, Les wrote a weekly satirical sports editorial called "The Games People Play" for the Long Island Graphic newspaper.

He currently resides in Florida with his wife Joy and counts his lucky stars that both of his children and their families live nearby.

This is his second novel.

www.ingramcontent.com/pod-product-compliance
Lightning Source LLC
Chambersburg PA
CBHW081540040426
42448CB00015B/3161